A STRAIGHTFORWARD GUIDE
TO DIVORCE AND THE LAW

ALEXANDER LOWTON

Straightforward Publishing Limited
38 Cromwell Road, London E17 9JN

©   Straightforward Publishing
     Second Edition 1996

British Library Cataloguing in Publication data. A catalogue record for
this book is available from the British Library.

ISBN 1 89992 455 8

Printed by BPC Wheaton – Exeter
Cover design by Neil Grant, Front Line Graphics,
Gerrard Street, Brighton.

CONTENTS

3 The Procedure for Obtaining a Divorce   25

4 Personal Protection in Your Home   33

5 Divorce and Children   43

6 Financial Support for Children   49

INTRODUCTION TO THIS BOOK

Those who have bothered to pick up this book will, in the main, be people who have experienced an initial separation from their partner and are now considering taking the first steps towards finalising divorce.

Everything associated with separation and divorce is usually traumatic and hurtful to those involved. This book does not attempt to deal with the more personal aspects of divorce, such as the sense of failure, and sense of loss. What it does do, however, is offer a practical guide to how the divorce process works on a legal level and how you can prepare yourself adequately for these final steps towards ending your marriage.

As you begin the process of getting divorced you may feel that, rather than go rushing immediately to a solicitor, you want to gain a clearer picture of what lies ahead and a background knowledge of the procedures involved. You might even want to do a lot of the work yourself, in order to keep costs down and to exercise more control.

Getting divorced will usually involve a lot more than simply obtaining a decree which announces that your marriage is over. There will, in most cases, be questions surrounding children, property, money etc. From this book you will gain an insight into the law surrounding the divorce process and also how these other matters are resolved.

The book is set out as follows:

Chapter one deals in a general way with the law concerning divorce. The main ground for divorce is discussed in depth, based on the notion of the 'irretrievable breakdown' of a marriage and the five 'facts' underlying this ground are also discussed.

Chapter two deals extensively with the practicalities of commencing divorce proceedings and discusses when it is advisable to use a solicitor. The likely cost of divorce is also discussed together with the type of help available to help meet your expenses.

Chapter three deals with the practical procedure for obtaining a divorce which should enable you to determine whether you can 'go it alone', or whether your divorce is likely to be complicated, requiring the help of a solicitor.

Chapter four deals with your safety and protection in your home whilst you are waiting for the divorce to be finalised. There are invaluable tips on what to do if your safety and wellbeing are undermined.

Chapter five deals with divorce and children and discusses your responsibilities under the Children Act of 1989 and also the different kinds of court orders available.

Chapter six deals with financial support for children and the role of the Child Support Agency in determining and administrating child maintenance following divorce.

Chapter seven deals with the thorny problem of divorce and financial arrangements, such as the division of family assets.

Chapter eight deals with longer-term financial arrangements and the role of the courts generally.

Chapter nine deals with other considerations following divorce such as re-marriage, tax position and amending your will.

Chapter ten sets out the Government's proposed changes to the divorce law which should come into force in the next eighteen months.

At the end of the book there is useful information concerning different agencies which can offer advice to those experiencing the trauma of divorce. In addition there is a list of useful addresses.

Although this book cannot offer you emotional support through what are often very difficult times, it can at least offer practical support and guidance to enable you to avoid problems in the future.

If you have any comments concerning the contents and information in this book please do not hesitate to contact Straightforward Publishing at: 38 Cromwell Road, Walthamstow, London E17 9JN.

1

SEEKING A DIVORCE
THE MAIN PRINCIPLES IN LAW

Divorce law has developed over the years through legislation made by Parliament and through the build up of 'precedents' (cases decided by the courts). However, in the last thirty years, there have been fundamental changes in the way society and the law have come to view divorce.

Modern divorce law recognises that 'irretrievable breakdown' of a marriage should be the one and only ground for divorce. This recognition signalled a move away from the idea of 'guilty parties' in divorce.

Before the introduction of the notion of irretrievable breakdown it was held that one party had to prove that the other party was guilty of destroying the marriage before divorce could be granted. The law is now much more flexible in its recognition of the breakdown of a marriage.

Since the present law was introduced, making it much easier to obtain divorce, the number of marriage breakdowns in Britain has risen significantly, with one in three couples in Britain filing for divorce. This is currently the highest rate in Europe.

There are a lot of problems associated with the law, and the role of those who make divorce law generally. The whole question of divorce law is under scrutiny, particularly the question of whether or not the law should attempt to keep marriages intact or whether it should seek to ease the transition to final separation without presenting unnecessary obstacles.

However, although we hear periodic announcements from different politicians on the importance of keeping the family unit intact, and by implication making it harder for people to divorce, the whole climate has changed over the years whereby the law now seems to be the facilitator of divorce as opposed to dictating whether or not people can get a divorce. There has also been a major shift in the law concerning children of divorcing couples. Under the Children Act of 1989 parents in divorce proceedings are encouraged to take the initiative and take matters into their own hands, making their own decisions concerning the child's life after divorce. The courts role has been greatly restricted. (See chapter 5)

The Child Support Act of 1991 has also dramatically changed the role of the courts in divorce proceedings. After April 1993, maintenance applications are no longer a matter for the courts but for a new government agency, the Child Support Agency, which assesses and determines applications for maintenance in accordance with a set formula (see chapter 6) The courts will now only deal with applications for maintenance in certain circumstances.

THE COURTS

Before looking at the law surrounding divorce in greater depth we should look briefly at the structure of the courts and how divorce law is administered.

County Courts

County Courts are local courts, usually found within towns and cities throughout England and Wales. These courts do not deal with criminal matters but they attempt to find solutions to virtually every other type of problem facing people in every day life. Such problems might be those that arise between businesses and their customers, between neighbours and between landlord and tenant, to name but a few.

Not all county courts are able to deal with divorce. Those that can are known as divorce county courts. In London, the equivalent of the divorce county court is known as the 'Divorce Registry' and is based in the Royal Courts of Justice in the Strand. Decisions concerning divorce cases, and subsequent orders, are made by judges and district judges. These people are appointed from the ranks of senior lawyers.

In addition to the judges there is also a large staff of officials who provide the administrative machinery of the courts. Like all administrators, they are the backbone of the operation.

The High Court

The majority of divorce cases will be heard in the County Courts. Sometimes, rarely, divorce cases need to be referred to the High Court. There are several sections of the High Court – the section responsible for divorce and other similar matters is known as the Family Division.

THE HEARING OF YOUR CASE

Hearings related to divorce cases are either in 'open court' or in 'chambers'. Proceedings in open court are heard in the court room itself. They are usually formal and members of the public are allowed to attend. However, most divorces are heard in chambers. These proceedings are private and the general public has no right to attend or listen. Only those people directly concerned with the case are allowed to attend.

THE GROUND FOR DIVORCE.

The first question facing couples who wish to divorce is whether or not they qualify at the outset to bring proceedings, i.e., what are the ground rules.

If one or other party wishes to file for divorce, the most basic requirement that must be fulfilled is that they should have been married for one year minimum. They must also be 'domiciled' in this country, i.e., England is regarded as their home. Alternatively, they must have been resident in England for a minimum of one year before the date on which proceedings are brought.

A court can halt proceedings of a divorce case in England if it would be better for the case to be heard in another country. Usually, the court would try to decide which country is the most appropriate, or with which country the divorcing couple are most closely associated.

EVIDENCE FOR DIVORCE – THE FIVE FACTS.

As we have seen, there is only one ground for granting a divorce, that is the irretrievable breakdown of marriage. Fundamentally, this means that your marriage has broken down to such a degree that it cannot be retrieved and the only solution is to end it legally (Matrimonial Causes Act 1973).

The spouse who requests a divorce is known as the 'petitioner'. The other party is known as the 'respondent'.

Although there is only one ground for divorce, the court has to be satisfied that there is clear evidence of one of the following five facts:

1. That the respondent has committed adultery and the petitioner cannot, or finds it intolerable to live with the respondent;
2. That the respondent has behaved in such a way that you cannot reasonably be expected to live with him or her;
3. That the respondent has deserted you for a continuous period of two years immediately before the presentation of your petition for divorce;
4. That parties to a marriage have lived apart for more than two years prior to filing for divorce and that there is no objection or defence to filing for divorce. This is known as the 'no fault' ground;

5. That parties to marriage have lived apart continuously five years prior to filing for divorce.

We shall now look at each of these 'five facts' in more depth.

1. Adultery

Quite simply, adultery is defined as heterosexual sex between one party to a marriage and someone outside the marriage. Oddly enough, because the law states quite clearly heterosexual sex, then gay or lesbian sex cannot (in theory) constitute adultery.

Adultery usually means that a 'full' sexual act has been committed so if there has not been penetration this will not be seen to be adulterous.

For adultery to be proved, an admission by the respondent or evidence of adultery is usually sufficient. The co-respondent need not be named in the divorce petition. If you do mention the name of the co-respondent involved in the adultery, that person is entitled to take part in the divorce proceedings in so far as they affect them. The court will provide the co-respondent with copies of all the relevant divorce papers and he or she will have the opportunity to confirm or deny anything said about him or her in the divorce proceedings.

Proving adultery is the first step. You then have to satisfy the courts that you find it intolerable to live with the respondent any further. However, it is not essential to prove that you find it intolerable to live with the respondent because of their adultery. It may be that your marriage has been unhappy for some time and that the adulterous act has proven to be the end.

If, after you discover the respondent's adultery, you continue to live together as man and wife for a continuous period of six months or more, you will not be able to rely on that instance of adultery as a reason for divorce. As long as the periods of living together after the adultery do not exceed six months in total, the courts will completely disregard them. This gives some room for attempts at reconciliation.

2. Unreasonable behaviour

Although 'unreasonable behaviour' is a commonly cited fact for divorce, in practice the court has stringent criteria which must be met before this is accepted. The law actually says that you must demonstrate that your spouse has behaved in such a way that you cannot reasonably be expected to continue to live with that person.

The court considering your case will look at the particular circumstances surrounding your situation and will then decide whether or not you should continue to tolerate your partners behaviour within marriage.

The main principle underlying unreasonable behaviour is that it is particular to your own situation and that it cannot be seen as relative to other peoples behaviour.

You must prove that the behaviour of your partner has gone well beyond the kind of day-to-day irritations that many people suffer and there is real reason to grant a divorce.

Examples of such behaviour range from continuous violence and threatening or intimidating behaviour to drunkenness, sexual perversions, neglect, and imposing unreasonable restrictions on another person.

3. Desertion

The fact that you must prove that your spouse has deserted you for a continuous period of two years can present difficulties.

If you are seeking a divorce on the basis of desertion, then your solicitor (if you have one) will need to check rigorously that you comply with the often complex requirements upon which a court will insist before granting a divorce.

In the main, desertion has arisen because of other associated problems within marriage, and therefore this factor can often be joined with others when applying for a divorce

The simplest form of desertion is when one person walks out on another for no apparent reason. Desertion, however, is not just a physical separation of husband and wife. It implies that the deserting party has rejected all the normal obligations associated with marriage.

Before desertion is proven a court will need to be satisfied of two things:

1. You must demonstrate that you and your spouse have been living separately for a continuous period of two years immediately before you started the divorce proceedings. Although it is usual for separation to start when one person leaves the marital home, it can also happen whilst you are living under the same roof, but living totally separate lives.

   The courts are very rigorous indeed when determining that this is the case and will need to be satisfied that your lives are indeed separate and that you can no longer go on carrying out functions jointly.

   The court will disregard short periods during the separation where you may have attempted to patch up your differences. However, if, for example, you attempt to reconcile six months into the initial two year period and this lasts for two months before you separate again, although the courts will not make you start again they will make you wait a further two months before they will hear your divorce. Therefore, the two years becomes two years and two months.

2. That your spouse has decided that your marriage is over – you must also be able to demonstrate that when he or she stopped living with you, your spouse viewed the marriage as ended and intended to separate from you on a permanent basis.

You will not be able to claim desertion if you consented to the separation. The court will take consent to mean that you made it clear from the outset that you consented to separation, through your words or actions.

In addition, you will not be able to claim desertion if your spouse had perfectly good reason to leave, for example he or she may have gone abroad with your full knowledge, to work or may have entered hospital for a long period.

If your spouse leaves because of your own unreasonable behaviour, then you cannot claim desertion. If you are to blame in this case, the courts will not accept desertion.

Finally, because the courts see desertion as essentially separation against your will, then if you come back together again on a permanent basis you can no longer claim desertion.

4. Separation for two years with consent

As with desertion, the particular circumstances in which the law looks upon you as having been separated for two years can include periods of time where you may have been under the same roof together but not functioning as a married couple. There may be short periods during this time where you have lived together, for example, in an attempt at reconciliation.

However, as with desertion you will not be able to count these periods towards the two years separation. Therefore, if you have a trial reconciliation period for three months then you will have to wait two years and three months before you can apply for divorce.

The basic difference between desertion and separation with consent is that you would not be granted a divorce on the basis of separation if your spouse did not give his or her consent to the divorce.

The court has rigid criteria for proving that your spouse consents to the divorce. Consent is only seen as valid if your spouse has freely given it without pressure. There must also be full understanding on his or her part of what a divorce will mean and how it will affect his or her life.

The court sends a form to divorcing parties soon after initial divorce papers are filed, together with explanatory notes and it is at this point when your spouse will give consent.

If your spouse will not consent to divorce and you cannot prove either desertion or adultery then you will be in the position where you will have to wait until five years separation has elapsed before you can seek a divorce.

In relation to the above, i.e., divorces granted on the basis of two years separation and consent or five years separation, the courts can exercise special powers to ensure that the financial and personal position of the respondent is protected. The courts can sometimes delay the process of divorce, or even prevent it, to make sure that there is no undue suffering or exploitation.

5. Five years separation

The last of the 'five facts' is that of five years separation. If you have been separated for five or more years the courts will grant a divorce whether or not the other party agrees to it, subject to what has been said above.

Again, the courts will allow for a period of attempted reconciliation up to six months and the rules concerning length of time apply, as with the other facts. Should you live together for longer than six months, the court will demand that you start the five year period again.

RECONCILIATION

In all the provisions of the law relating to each of the five facts which have to be demonstrated in order to give evidence of the ground of 'irretrievable breakdown', there are built-in provisions for reconciliation. The law is fairly flexible when taking into account attempts at reconciling and sorting out differences.

In effect, these built-in provisions allow for a period of up to six months in which both parties can make a concerted attempt to solve their problems. If these attempts are unsuccessful then their legal position vis-a-vis divorce proceedings will not be jeopardized. The reconciliation provisions apply for a period up to six months or separate periods not exceeding six months.

In addition to this, a solicitor, if you have one, will need to certify that he or she has discussed the possibility of reconciliation with you and has ensured that both parties know where to seek advice and guidance if they really wish to attempt reconciliation.

The court, if it so wishes, can also adjourn proceedings to give both parties further time to decide whether they genuinely wish to make a further effort to continue their marriage.

At the end of this book names and addresses of various organisations which can help with the process of reconciliation are given. The most well known of these is RELATE.

CONCILIATION AND MEDIATION SERVICES

There is an essential difference between reconciliation which means sorting out differences and staying together, and those services which offer help through conciliation and mediation services. Conciliation is directed towards making parting easier to handle. The role of the conciliator is to sort out at least some of the difficulties between those who have made a definite and firm decision to obtain a divorce.

The process of conciliation can take place either out of court, or in court. In-court conciliation only arises once the process of litigating for divorce has commenced. It is particularly relevant where the future of children is under discussion.

With in-court conciliation, there is usually what is known as a 'pre-trial' review of the issues and problems which parties to a divorce are unable to settle themselves. Both the court welfare officer and the district judge are involved in this process.

Out-of-court conciliation and mediation are intended to assist both parties in reaching an agreement before they arrive in court or approach the court. The person involved at this stage is usually professionally trained, normally a social worker, who will act as go-between.

Both parties can also use specially trained legal personnel, lawyers to help them reach an agreement. This process is like the process of arbitration and is intended to make the formal legal proceedings less hostile and acrimonious.

For further information concerning useful addresses with regard to the family and law please refer to Appendix A.

In the next chapter, I will be dealing with the actual commencement of divorce proceedings following your decision to take action to end your marriage.

Now please read the KEY POINTS from chapter 1 overleaf.

KEY POINTS

- 'Irretrievable breakdown' is the one and only ground for divorce.

- Divorce proceedings are started in the Divorce County Court. The vast majority of cases are heard in the County Courts although a few are heard in the High Court.

- Hearings related to divorce cases are either in 'open court' or are heard in 'chambers'.

- The most basic requirement when filing for a divorce is that couples should have been married for one year.

- You must be 'domiciled' or live in the country where you apply for a divorce.

- Although the only ground for divorce is 'irretrievable breakdown', evidence of one of the 'five facts' (page 8) must be proven.

- In all the provisions of the law relating to the five facts, there are in-built provisions for reconciliation.

2

COMMENCING DIVORCE PROCEEDINGS

USING A SOLICITOR

Although it makes sense to take legal advice when taking your first steps towards divorce, there is no rule to say that you have to.

The amount of advice you will need from a solicitor will depend entirely on the circumstances of your case and the complexities involved. One of the reasons for reading a book such as this is to broaden your knowledge and put yourself in a stronger position to handle proceedings.

Most divorces will have two fairly distinct stages – the first step of obtaining the divorce decree (divorce) and the more complicated problems of sorting out property and financial matters and making arrangements concerning children.

As with most county court procedures nowadays, the procedure for commencing divorce and the subsequent steps up to the issuing of a decree are largely paperwork. Provided that the circumstances of your divorce are straightforward then there is no real need to consult a solicitor at all. In the next chapter, I will be discussing the actual procedure and how to obtain a divorce without a solicitor.

It is up to each party to ascertain the complexity of the divorce before deciding to go it alone. The question you should be asking yourselves, preferably during a face-to-face meeting, is whether or not the marriage can be ended with the minimum of problems.

If you are childless and there is no property at stake and there will be no financial complications then you should be able to proceed without a solicitor.

If, however, you own property, and have children, and also have life insurance policies and pension schemes etc., then you will need to try to reach agreement concerning the division of these. This is where divorce gets complicated and you may feel you need legal advice.

The division of your assets is a matter for you both but it has to be reached by agreement. I will be discussing financial matters and children later in the book.

One other aspect of do-it-yourself divorce is that it can be time-consuming. Some people do not have available the large amount of time it would involve and will be happier to leave it to a solicitor.

A solicitor will handle the whole matter for you, once instructed, from eliciting initial information from you to obtaining a decree from the court. Your main input will be to check over the necessary paperwork at each stage, as required and, in certain cases to deliver documents to the court. However, all of this will be done at the request and direction of the solicitor

YOUR FUTURE ARRANGEMENTS

Whilst it is not essential to consult a solicitor, it is wise to at least get a view on future arrangements which you have negotiated. This is particularly important when it comes to future tax arrangements.

If it is necessary to ask a court to determine future arrangements, because of the inability of parties to a divorce to agree or negotiate, then a solicitor will need to take charge of the whole process. Remember, the more a solicitor does for you the more it will cost. You should both bear this in mind when beginning discussions.

YOUR CHOICE OF SOLICITOR

Not all solicitors deal with divorce cases, as this is a specialised area of the law. In addition, not all solicitors operate the 'Green Form' scheme (see below) which provides for legal aid.

It is always best for parties to a divorce to use separate solicitors over divorce. Solicitors, in the main would prefer to represent one party and not both as this can present certain conflicts of loyalty and interest, particularly where there are antagonisms.

The first task is for you to choose a solicitor. This can be done either by consulting business pages or, perhaps better, choosing from a list of recommended solicitors which you can obtain from an advice agency, such as the Citizens' Advice Bureau.

You may also feel that you will be eligible for legal aid and you should ensure the firm of solicitors that you choose operates this. Solicitors who do operate under legal aid will be marked on the list of firms – solicitors offices often clearly demonstrate their participation in the scheme by a sign showing two people sitting at a table with the words 'legal aid' underneath.

When you have decided on a firm of solicitors, you should then contact them to make an initial appointment to discuss the matter. Your decision to allow a firm to act for you is a commercial one, and you will want in the initial stages to determine the costs and timeframe for your divorce. As there are a number of firms you should at first test the market in order to ensure that you are getting the best deal.

HOW MUCH WILL IT COST?

Although the cost of using a solicitor can be quite high, you should be able to keep the overall expense to a reasonable level. You may be eligible for help under the 'Green Form' scheme, as mentioned above.

THE GREEN FORM SCHEME

Both parties to a divorce may be able to benefit from the Green Form Scheme. Its availability is not limited to one party. The main principle behind any form of legal aid is that it is means tested, and depends on your income.

The levels of income for eligibility for legal aid change frequently and you can check these with any firm of solicitors which operates this scheme. Like many means tested benefits, if you are in receipt of benefits such as income support then you will almost certainly qualify for aid.

Tables of earnings levels which qualify for the Green Form scheme can be obtained from HMSO (Her Majesty's Stationery Office) or from any Citizens' Advice Bureau or Law Centre.

When you first see a solicitor, you will be told straightaway if you qualify for assistance. The eventual cost to you will vary from nil cost to a partial contribution to payment of the whole amount.

However, it is as well to bear in mind that, even if you have not contributed towards, the scheme you may be asked to reimburse the legal aid fund at a later date, from anything that you may gain as a result of the divorce, such as cash or property. You should certainly ask your solicitor to make it clear how much you may have to reimburse.

If there are other matters to be sorted out, such as property and children you may also be entitled to go on and receive legal aid, which is rather different to the Green Form Scheme but is also means tested. The table from HMSO indicates eligibility.

The Green Form Scheme will, normally, entitle you to advice and help in relation to your divorce. The only things that it does not cover are the costs of attendance at court by the solicitor acting on your behalf. Therefore, any court appointments to discuss arrangements with a judge will need to be attended by yourself.

If you feel you need to obtain more information concerning the divorce procedure and a solicitor's involvement then you should be able to obtain a Fixed Fee Interview with a solicitor to discuss the matter. This is separate from help and assistance under the Green Form Scheme and is intended to provide you with a clear framework for the future proceedings. Again, a number of advice agencies, such as the Citizens' Advice Bureau, will be able to provide you with a list of solicitors who provide this service.

If you are unable to receive any help whatsoever from the Green Form Scheme, or from legal aid then it is really necessary for you to consider the possible future outlay. Solicitors are not cheap, they charge for time incurred but you should also be able to operate for a fixed fee plus any outgoings. It is a bit like buying a house in that you pay for a set service. The costs go upwards the more complicated your case. Do not be afraid to ask exactly how much you can expect to be charged.

RECOVERING THE COST OF DIVORCE FROM YOUR SPOUSE

It is wise to agree between you beforehand who will pay what costs towards the divorce. One of the fundamental principles when handling divorce is to try to sort as much out as possible at the beginning in order to minimise future complications and also costs, both emotional and financial.

If you cannot decide, or agree, the court will take a view as to who should bear costs. As a general rule, the petitioner will hardly ever be ordered to pay the respondents costs of divorce. A respondent, however, may have to pay a petitioners costs, although not if the petitioner is eligible under the Green Form Scheme. This depends entirely on the basis for divorce.

You can change your solicitor at any time if you are unhappy and are paying for the service out of your own pocket. However, you will have to settle your solicitors bill up to that point. If you feel that you have a complaint about the service you have received you can complain to the Solicitors' Complaints Bureau, set up by the Law Society as part of its regulatory functions. Any advice agency will give you details concerning the Solicitors' Complaints Bureau and how to go about complaining.

If you are receiving benefits under the Green Form Scheme then your right to change solicitors is more restricted. However, if you are very dissatisfied then you will usually be able to change solicitors. You should find another solicitor and explain the circumstances. He or she will then arrange to take your case on.

Do not forget that it is very important for you to sort out as many problems as possible before consulting a solicitor. The more questions you can deal with in advance the less problematic will be the divorce and in consequence the less will be the cost to you – particularly important to you if you are meeting it out of your own pocket.

In addition, the clearer the picture when you do eventually commence divorce proceedings the smoother the transition to obtaining your decree will be.

In the next chapter I will be describing the steps towards obtaining a divorce and how to do it yourself. It is a question of paperwork and procedure and if arrangements are not too complicated there is every reason to be confident that you can obtain your own divorce – without the unnecessary involvement of a solicitor.

Now please read the KEY POINTS from chapter 2 opposite.

KEY POINTS

- Provided the circumstances of your divorce are straightforward, there is no real need to use a solicitor.

- More complicated divorces will almost certainly require the use of a solicitor.

- You may want to get a view concerning your long-term arrangements even if you do not use a solicitor.

- It is always best for parties to a divorce to use separate solicitors.

- Once you have chosen to use a solicitor you may be eligible for financial help through the 'Green Form' scheme or through Legal Aid.

- It is wise to agree beforehand, with your spouse, who will pay what costs towards the divorce. If you cannot agree, the court will take a view as to who should pay.

3

THE PROCEDURE
FOR OBTAINING A DIVORCE

In an undefended petition, both spouses accept that the divorce will go ahead. In a defended petition, one spouse objects to the divorce and is filing a defence against the petition.

A special procedure was introduced to deal with undefended divorce petitions, primarily because of the large volume of cases presented to the courts.

At present, there is a set pattern which you must follow if you wish to obtain a divorce and the case is undefended:

a) the petition (a prescribed form) must be filled in;
b) the petition must enclose a 'statement of arrangements' for the children;
c) the petition must be sent to the registrar of the divorce county court;
d) there must be sufficient copies for the other parties to the divorce;
e) the respondent will then receive his or her copies from the court;
f) other parties involved will receive their copies;
g) the respondent must, on a prescribed form, acknowledge service;
h) the respondent must make clear that he or she has no intention to defend;

i) the documents are examined by a court official (the divorce registrar);
j) the divorce registrar then certifies that the facts of the case are proven;
k) the judge pronounces the decree nisi in open court;
l) the decree is made absolute on application by the petitioner.

It is important to remember that, following the granting of a decree nisi in court, your divorce isn't final until a minimum period of six weeks has passed when it is made absolute.

Each of the above steps will be discussed briefly below.

THE PREPARATION OF THE DIVORCE PETITION

Either you or your solicitor will prepare the divorce petition. This document can be obtained from HMSO and will form the basis of your claim for a divorce.

On this form you will record details of your marriage and your children and the grounds on which you are seeking a divorce. You will also list the claims you are asking the court to consider. This part is particularly important. For example, you may wish the court to consider financial matters for you.

Normally, you would include your address on the form but you can make application to the court to leave out your address if this poses any danger to you.

It is of the utmost importance that you take care in filling in the form because you are asking the court to make a very important decision on the basis of information given. You should avoid exaggerating the truth.

THE STATEMENT OF ARRANGEMENTS

If there are children involved you must fill in another document known simply as the 'statement of arrangements for children' This sets out the arrangements you intend to make for children once the divorce is granted.

A child, for the purposes of the court is any child who is a child of both parties, an adopted child, or any other child who has been treated by both as part of the family. This does not include children boarded out by local authorities or social services or other voluntary organisations.

Although the courts are not generally concerned with the welfare of adult children (over sixteen) you will be required to give details of children under eighteen who are still receiving instruction at an educational establishment or undergoing other training such as for trade or profession.

The information required for the statement of arrangements will be:

a) where the children will live after divorce;
b) who else will be residing there;
c) who will look after them;
d) where they are to be educated;
e) what financial arrangements have been proposed for them;
f) what arrangements have been made for the other parent to see them;
g) whether they have any illness or disability;
i) whether they are under the care or supervision of a person or organisation (i.e. social services).

When you have completed this form your spouse should be in agreement. If she or he is not then there will be an opportunity at a later stage to make alternative proposals to the court.

FILING THE PAPERS WITH THE COURT

The court office requires the following to commence proceedings:

a) the completed divorce petition (plus copy for spouse);
b) completed statement of arrangements if appropriate (plus copy for spouse);
c) a copy of your marriage certificate;
d) in certain cases, a fee if you are not receiving help under the Green Form Scheme;

e) a reference number which will be given once the case is received by the court.

SERVING THE PAPERS ON THE RESPONDENT AND CO-RESPONDENT

Once the petition has been received by the courts, the court office will send a copy, plus a copy of the statement of arrangements, to the respondent. This is known as 'serving' the documents on the respondent. He or she will also receive two other documents from the court – the 'acknowledgement of service' and the 'notice of proceedings'.

The notice of proceedings informs the respondent that divorce proceedings have been commenced against him or her and that person must acknowledge service within eight days. There are further instructions concerning seeking legal help or filing an acknowledgement personally.

This document, the acknowledgement of service, is self-explanatory and is designed in question & answer form. It is designed to assure the court that the respondent has received the papers and is fully aware of impending divorce proceedings against them. The court will not proceed with the case until it has received this information.

If you have commenced proceedings on the ground of adultery then the third party, who is known as the co-respondent, is entitled to be notified of the divorce proceedings.

NON-DEFENCE OF DIVORCE PROCEEDINGS

Where the respondent does not wish to defend proceedings, the next steps should be quite straightforward. The court will send either you or your solicitor a copy of the completed acknowledgement of service together with copies of two more forms known as 'request for directions for trial' (special procedure) and the 'affidavit of evidence' (special procedure). The special procedure indicates that the divorce process will be streamlined. In the past, all petitioners seeking a divorce had to go to court and give evidence before a judge. This is no longer necessary. Like many county court procedures the route is now simplified and quicker.

The affidavit of evidence, like all affidavits, confirms that what you have said in your petition is true. You will need to take an oath in front of a solicitor which is called 'swearing' the affidavit. Any questions concerning the truth later could ultimately, if it is discovered that you have lied, lead to your being found guilty of contempt of court.

The 'request for directions for trial' is a basic form requesting the court to proceed with your case. Both documents, the affidavit and the request for directions are then returned to the court.

The case is then examined by an official of the court who will either declare that whether or not the facts of the case are proven.

If the district judge is happy with the case he or she will issue a certificate saying that you are entitled to a decree of divorce. Any claims for costs will also be considered at this stage.

When a certificate has been issued, a date will be fixed for decree nisi to be pronounced in open court by judge or district judge. You will be informed of this date but you need not attend court. However, if there is a dispute over costs you will need to attend and the matter will be dealt with by the judge

Both the respondent and petitioner are then sent a copy of the decree nisi by the court. However, you have not yet reached the stage of being finally divorced. It is only when your divorce has been made absolute at a later stage that you will be free to remarry if you wish. A decree absolute follows no less than six weeks after decree nisi.

If the district judge is not satisfied that you should be granted a divorce, then you will either be asked to produce further evidence or the matter will be sent for trial. This rarely happens. You may be entitled to legal aid if this does happen. This is dependent on your income and you should seek advice. If you are refused a divorce, and you have been handling the case yourself then you will most certainly need to go and see a solicitor.

DEFENCE OF DIVORCE PROCEEDINGS

If the respondent or co-respondent has returned the papers stating that he or she intends to defend the petition, your next move will be very much dependent on whether an 'answer' setting out the defence has been filed. The respondent has twenty-nine days to file a reply.

If a defence has been filed, the special procedure designed to speed up the process can no longer be used. In this case it is advisable to see a solicitor. There will eventually be a date given for a hearing in court at which both the petitioner and respondent will be expected to attend.

Evidence will be given to the judge who will then have to decide if a divorce should be granted. Legal aid would almost certainly be available if you are financially eligible. The whole process, depending on the defence, can be quite lengthy.

If you are the respondent and you feel that you wish to defend the petition you will almost certainly need to see a solicitor and take advice. In general, undefended straightforward cases, particularly where there are no children involved, can be done on a do-it-yourself basis. Anything more complicated will mean that you will probably need to see a solicitor.

If any other problems arise, such as the respondent either failing or refusing to return acknowledgement of service, proceedings will be delayed whilst a visit by a court official is made. This visit is to ascertain and provide evidence of service.

If the respondent cannot be traced, a request can be made to the court for the petition to be heard anyway. Again, this will result in delay.

POSSIBLE CHANGES TO THE LAW

The present state of the law surrounding divorce is seen as unsatisfactory. This applies to the law itself and also the special procedure outlined above.

As we have discussed, the debate concerning divorce law, and the role of the lawmakers, is intense and is intricately bound up with morality and politics.

In particular, the current debate concerning the status of one-parent families and also the breakdown of the family unit is having an effect on the shape and form that divorce law will take.

The following are some of the proposals under discussion which may eventually be translated into legislation:

- there will be no need to prove any of the 'five facts';
- the couple must demonstrate, however, that there has been a period of consideration of the practical arrangements following divorce;
- such period will last one year;
- the couple do not have to be separated during this period;
- the period of a year will date from when one or both of the spouses files a sworn statement to the court that in his or her belief the marriage has broken down;
- conciliation will be available. It is being suggested that a couple will be bound to make use of a family advice centre as their first port of call. They will then be directed to conciliation, mediation, counselling or to lawyers as needed.

These ideas are under review and it will be a while before they are translated into legislation.

For further information concerning useful addresses please refer to Appendix B.

Now please read the KEY POINTS from chapter 3 overleaf.

KEY POINTS

• In an undefended divorce petition, both spouses agree that the divorce will go ahead. In a defended petition, one spouse objects to the divorce and will file a defence against the petition.

• There are a number of set steps that you must take if you wish to obtain a divorce and the case is undefended. These are listed on page 25. Careful reading should enable you to carry out your own divorce proceedings without the use of a solicitor.

• There may, in the future, be significant changes to the law of divorce following a review of the whole procedure.

4

PERSONAL PROTECTION IN YOUR HOME

If you are fortunate, you and your spouse may be able to part without animosity when you realise that your marriage is over. However, it is just as likely that you will have to remain under the same roof even though your personal relationships may be tense and strained. In many cases, when your marriage starts to break down so each of you will try to torment the other, to a degree not seen during happier times.

There are many things to consider if relationships start to deteriorate. If you have children the considerations will become more urgent. One of the main issues will be that of who moves out? Who takes care of the children, how will you get them to school and so on.

The courts are able to help with these sorts of considerations, and this chapter outlines the various powers of the court to help you until matters are sorted out.

HOW TO GET HELP FROM THE COURT

Help is available either from the county court or the magistrates' court. Both husband and wife are equally entitled to help from the court, although it is more usual for the wife to seek help. In some cases, it may be more appropriate for each of you to ask the court to intervene in some way.

It is not necessary for either of you to have started divorce proceedings before you apply, nor essential that you are still living together. Neither does it matter who owns the house nor whose name it is in.

HELP FROM THE MAGISTRATES' COURT

The magistrates' court can make orders protecting you or a child of the family from your spouse. These are called 'personal protection orders'. Before you can get a personal protection order, you will have to satisfy the court of the following:

- that your spouse has used violence or threatened to use violence against you and a child of the family and;
- that you need to be protected from him/her by an order of the court.

If you can satisfy these conditions, the court can make an order preventing your spouse from using or threatening violence against you and/or your family.

The magistrates' court can also make an order excluding your spouse from your home. This is called an 'exclusion order'. The magistrates will only make an exclusion order if your case is serious.

If your spouse has already been violent towards you or a child of the family, you must be able to show that you or the child are in danger of being physically injured by him/her, or would be if he were to be allowed into the home.

If your spouse has not actually been violent towards you or a child yet, you will have to demonstrate:

- that you or a child are in danger of being physically injured by him/her and;
- that he/she has threatened you or a child with violence and by doing so he was breaking an existing personal protection order already in force, or alternatively, that he/she has threatened you or a child with violence, and he/she has already demonstrated that

they are capable of violent behaviour by using violence on someone else.

If necessary, when it makes an exclusion order the court can also order your spouse to allow you to return to live in the home. This might be appropriate, for example, if there was a serious risk that your spouse would move out as directed but at the same time change all the locks so that you could not get back into the property.

HELP FROM THE COUNTY COURT

There is a wide range of orders available from the county court. They fall into two categories; 'non-molestation orders' and 'exclusion orders'. The technical name for an order of either type is an injunction.

Non-molestation injunctions

The court can make an order prohibiting your spouse from molesting you or your children. This order is roughly the equivalent of the magistrates personal protection order, although the county court is able to protect you not only from violence but from a wider range of behaviour on the part of your spouse.

Exclusion injunctions

The court can exclude your spouse from the family home and even from the immediate vicinity of the house and can also order him/her to permit you to return to live there if he/she has turned you out, or is preventing you from entering.

The court will not make this sort of order lightly. It must be fair, just and reasonable to do so. There are many factors to be taken into account including the behaviour of each of you, and both your personal circumstances – for instance what, if any, alternative accommodation you would each be able to find if you had to leave, whether either of you will suffer injury to your physical or mental health if you have to go on living in the same house, and so on.

If you have children, the court will concentrate particularly on how the situation is affecting them. It will want to know how much it is distressing the children to see the relationship between you and your spouse deteriorate, what effect it would have on them if your spouse was ordered to leave and how they would be affected if he/she was to stay; whether they are, in fact, being directly involved in the breakdown of your marriage, perhaps because your spouse has threatened violence towards them.

When the court has all the information necessary, it is likely to approach its decision on the house in two parts. It will first decide whether the situation has got so bad that you can no longer go on living together as a family in the same house. If it considers that this is so, it has then got to decide how things can be arranged so that you and your spouse do not come into contact any more than is necessary. If your house is small then the court may have no choice but to order you both out. If you have more room, it may be possible for the court to divide up the house and allocate part to each of you so you both have separate space.

If you have children, the court's decision will usually be determined by what is going to happen to the children. The parent who is going to look after them will normally be allowed to stay in the house while the other will have to move out.

If there are no children, the court will decide what should be done by looking at the way you have both behaved and assessing which of you would be better able to fend for yourself if turned out of your home. If one of you has obviously behaved far more unreasonably than the other, that person can usually expect to be the one asked or ordered to leave.

If there is a serious possibility of your spouse making a nuisance of himself/herself in the vicinity of the house at any time after he/she has been ordered to leave, the court can be asked to make a further order prohibiting him/her from coming within a specified distance of the house.

As with a non-molestation injunction, it is worth remembering that an exclusion injunction will not be granted unless there is real reason.

If you are asking the court for such an order you will have to attend court to give evidence about your circumstances, and you may also have to swear an affidavit setting out in writing why you need the courts help. Your spouse will also usually have the opportunity to give evidence at the court hearing.

It is up to the court to decide how long its order should last. It will generally specify the duration of the order when it makes it

Personal protection orders and non-molestation injunctions will generally last until you are divorced although the court can grant an injunction for a shorter or longer period. Exclusion orders and injunctions do not generally last for as long as the above orders. They are not intended to resolve the question of your accommodation for good but to tide you over until you can make alternative arrangements or take divorce proceedings so that the court has an opportunity to deal with long term arrangements for your family property.

If either party wants the terms of the order or the injunction discharged completely you are free to ask the court to make a further order.

LIVING TOGETHER WHILST THE COURT ORDER IS IN FORCE

Non-molestation injunctions and personal protection orders do not necessarily mean that you will be living separately; they simply regulate your conduct towards each other. An exclusion order will mean that you will be living apart. However, if you both want to give things another try and start living together again, you are perfectly free to do so without referring to the court.

If this is the case and your spouse feels that he/she would rather not have the exclusion order hanging over him/her then he/she can apply to the court to have it discharged.

SEEING THE CHILDREN WHEN THE COURT ORDER IS IN FORCE

Provided that your spouse has not been specifically prevented by the court from seeing the children he/she will normally be entitled to do so even though a personal protection order or non-molestation order is in force or he/she has been excluded from the home. However, you may have to be prepared to alter your arrangements over contact to make sure that they do not involve your spouse breaking the court order.

HOW QUICKLY CAN YOU GET AN ORDER?

In a normal case, the court will not deal with your application until your spouse has been notified of it and given a chance to attend at court to put his/her side of the story. If you urgently need help because you or a child of the family are in imminent danger of being seriously injured by your spouse, the court can immediately act without your spouse even knowing that you have made an application. If the court makes an emergency application in this way, the order is described as an 'ex parte order' in the county court and in the magistrates' court it is described as an 'expedited order'.

As a general rule, you will not be able to obtain an exclusion order by this emergency procedure – the only protection you will be given will be in the form of a non-molestation order or personal protection order. In a really urgent case, it is possible to apply to a judge of the county court for an injunction, even outside court hours, but this is not possible in the magistrates' court which can only deal with applications during court time.

An emergency order will only be temporary. In the county court, it will last until the earliest possible date when the whole case can be considered in full with an opportunity for your spouse to have his/her say.

An order of the magistrates' court made in an emergency can only last for a maximum of twenty-eight days, even if there has not been an

4 PERSONAL PROTECTION IN YOUR HOME

opportunity for a full investigation of the case before then. However, you can apply for it to be renewed at the end of the twenty-eight day period.

The time actually taken to obtain an order, either in an emergency or in the normal way, will depend on all the circumstances – not only what your case involves but also how busy the court is.

UNDERTAKINGS TO THE COURT

If you have made an application to the county court, and your spouse is willing to promise that he/she will not molest you or will move out of the house within a certain length of time he/she may give the court an undertaking that this will be the case. Breach of this undertaking can mean heavy penalties.

ENFORCING A COURT ORDER

If the court order is not obeyed, then the next step in the process depends very much whether or not there is a 'power of arrest' within the court order. This is a special order entitling the police to arrest your spouse straightaway if he/she breaks the court order. If the court makes an order prohibiting your spouse from using violence towards you or a child of the family or excluding him/her from the home, and it is satisfied that he/she has already injured you or a child of the family, it can grant a power of arrest.

If a power of arrest is granted with your order, and your spouse breaks the courts order by using violence towards you or the child or by entering the house or the surrounding area after he/she has been excluded, you should contact your local police station. The police will normally arrest your spouse at once. If he/she is arrested, he/she will be kept in custody and brought before the court within twenty-four hours.

The court will have to decide what should be done about your spouse's conduct. It can send him/her immediately to prison for whatever period it thinks appropriate. However, this is unlikely to happen if it is the first time he/she has broken the injunction or order, as imprisonment is usually reserved as something of a last resort for people who have persistently disobeyed the courts orders. Alternatively, the court can fine your spouse.

In addition to the above, there are other measures that the court can take. For example, the court may decide to modify the original order in the light of what has happened. If you are not granted a power of arrest, it is up to you, with your solicitors help, to take steps to bring your spouse back to court if he/she breaks the order so that the court can decide what is to be done.

The proceedings described so far in this chapter are 'civil proceedings', in other words, they do not involve a criminal prosecution. However, if your spouse assaults you or damages your property, he/she will have committed a criminal offence. The police would be reluctant to take action, though, without a power of arrest.

If you are dissatisfied that the police are not prosecuting your spouse, you may be able to bring a criminal prosecution against him/her yourself. You should, however, think carefully before going down this road because of the stress and the expense.

Now please read the KEY POINTS from chapter 4 opposite.

KEY POINTS

• If you are experiencing problems in your home following the breakdown of your marriage, you can get help from the county courts or the magistrates' courts.

• The county court can grant a wide range of orders such as 'non-molestation' orders and 'exclusion' orders. The technical name for an order of this type is an injunction.

• The magistrates' court can make orders protecting you and your children. These are called 'personal protection' orders and 'exclusion' orders.

• If an order is violated this can ultimately lead to imprisonment for contempt of court.

5

DIVORCE AND CHILDREN

When considering a divorce petition, it is the duty of a court to have regard to all the circumstances within that petition but the first, and possibly most important consideration, will be the welfare of any children in the family under the age of eighteen years old.

The practice of the courts prior to 1989 was to make orders regulating where the children of a divorced family were to live (known as a custody order) and what contact each parent would have with that child (access order) but the Children Act of 1989 has changed all this.

THE CHILDREN ACT OF 1989

The underlying aim, of the Children Act of 1989 is that where there is marital breakdown the law should play as small a role as possible. Parents must continue to care for and to have responsibility for their children until they reach the age of eighteen.

As far as possible, when divorce proceedings are in progress, parents should make their own decisions concerning a child's welfare. The new act therefore seeks to minimize the court's role in final decisions.

However, should you decide to seek assistance from the courts, the

Children Act of 1989 provides a range of orders which can, if necessary, be used to resolve issues relating to children. The old custody and access orders have been replaced by four main types of order. The terms now used are felt to be more appropriate:

1. Residence orders – these orders settle the arrangements as to where a child will live. Although this will normally be with one of the parents, third parties, such as relatives can apply for a residence order.
2. Contact orders – these regulate the contact that child will have with the person named in the order.
3. Prohibited steps order – this prohibits a parent from exercising his/ her parental responsibility for a child in whatever way is stipulated in the order, that is, a parent could be prohibited from bringing a child into contact with an undesirable person named in the order.
4. Specific issue order – this decides a particular issue which has arisen in connection with any aspect of parental responsibility for a child. One example could be where a child is to be educated.

It should be noted that a court has the power to make an order under the Children Act wherever one is necessary, whether or not divorce proceedings have commenced. If a petition for divorce has already been filed, the county court will almost certainly deal with the application. In other situations however, an application can be made to a magistrates' court instead.

Because the Children Act has fundamentally changed the way the courts view the responsibility for children's welfare following divorce we shall look at two of the orders in a little more detail.

RESIDENCE ORDERS

If you and your spouse can reach agreement concerning where a child will live after the divorce, then the courts will not intervene. If you cannot reach agreement, a residence order will be made.

Whatever requirement the residence order stipulates, you will both continue to have parental responsibility for the children.

Although the parent with whom the child lives will go on making day-to-day decisions for the child the other parent has a right to participate in basic decisions such as education, etc. If disagreement arises over these matters one or other of the parents can seek a specific issue order or a prohibited steps order.

The most common type of residence order is for children to live with one parent and see the other parent regularly, for purposes of keeping contact.

The most usual situation is for the mother to be the parent and for the father to have regular contact. A residence order can be made in favour of more than one person where the circumstances warrant it. For example, a residence order can be granted to a woman and new spouse.

If there are problems in issuing residence orders in the beginning, a court can issue a temporary order to regulate the situation, known as an interim order. This is rare, but the courts do have the powers.

THE PROCEDURE FOR A RESIDENCE ORDER

Again, as with most county court procedures, the first step in applying for a residence order is to fill in the appropriate form setting out details about yourself and also details concerning the type of order you are seeking.

This form is then served on the other parent who will file it with the court and serve on you a brief answer as to the proposals. The court will give directions on how the matter will proceed. If you have any witnesses supporting your case for the order, it is highly likely that you will have to inform them that they may have to attend court to give evidence. If you have a solicitor acting for you then that person will request details.

It is likely that if matters start to become complicated then you will be using a solicitor.

In most cases the court will also seek an independent report about your case to help it reach a decision. This would be prepared by a welfare officer or another person from an agency experienced in these matters.

The solicitor representing you will ask for a copy of the independent report before the hearing of your case in order to ensure that you agree with the contents.

After the court has received all the evidence it needs and you have attended court, the order that the judge makes is usually intended to be long term. However, a residence order is never absolutely final (it can't be) and can be altered if circumstances make this necessary.

The underlying principle guiding any judge's decision is that the welfare of the child must come first.

When a residence order has been made and is in force, the law provides that no person shall be allowed to change the surname of that child without the consent of everyone with parental responsibility, or leave of the court.

If the other parent will not consent to a change of name then you will have to make application to the court and convince the judge that there is good reason to change the name.

If you wish to take your child abroad and a residence order has been made, the written consent of every person with parental responsibility, or leave of the court, is needed. The only exception to this rule is that the person in whose favour an order has been made can take the child abroad for less than one month.

CONTACT ORDERS

The court will expect both parties to agree as to what is reasonable contact in your own particular case. If you can't reach agreement the court will decide what is reasonable in your case and will define when contact should take place.

The court will take a fairly stringent view concerning contact and will, if there is strong evidence that it is not in the interests of a child, ensure that contact is prevented. However, the court will only do this in quite exceptional circumstances. Normally, notwithstanding the emotions surrounding applications to restrict contact, the court will act in the best interests of the child.

If you are making application for the child to stay overnight with the contact parent, the court will only agree if suitable accommodation is provided. If the child genuinely does not wish to stay overnight then a court is unlikely to make such an order.

If the court is worried about arrangements for contact then it can sometimes arrange for supervised contact visits, to make sure that everything is all right. If this proves to be the case, supervision will cease.

Some areas have family centres where contact visits can take place with family centre workers in waiting to assist transfer of the child from one parent to another, to ensure that problems do not arise.

Like a residence order, a contact order is never final. This is because individual circumstances change and you may need to ask the court to reconsider the order and the provisions made.

It is obviously much easier if both parents agree on the nature of contact, avoiding the need for an order. You should think very carefully about the arrangements and take into account days such as birthdays, Christmas Day, etc. It is during these times that each parent will want contact and you should try to agree on a framework which will minimise possibilities of emotional upset.

Now please read the KEY POINTS from chapter 5 overleaf.

KEY POINTS

- The Children Act 1989 regulates the contact between parents of children following divorce.

- The underlying aim of the Children Act is that where there is marital breakdown the law should play as small a role as possible.

- There are four main types of order provided for by the Children Act: residence orders; contact orders; prohibited steps orders; and specific issue orders.

- These orders will only be enforced by the courts if divorced couples cannot agree concerning the welfare of children.

6

FINANCIAL SUPPORT FOR CHILDREN

THE CHILD SUPPORT ACT 1991

The question of paying for the upkeep of children following divorce is an extremely important one indeed. The government has taken a close look at the number of parents not keeping to maintenance agreements and to reflect its conclusions has introduced fundamental changes to the law.

Since the Child Support Act 1991 came into force in April 1993, children's maintenance in divorce proceedings has been assessed by the Child Support Agency. The courts will no longer decide on questions of financial provision for children unless:

- the payments exceed the amount assessed by the agency or
- there are special grounds put forward such as educational needs.

In addition:

- the courts will still have jurisdiction to make orders for stepchildren and other children of the family;
- the courts will still make orders for lump sum and property adjustment orders for children;
- the court will still make orders for disabled children.

The Child Support Agency, which will operate the system of assessment of maintenance (and enforcement) applies to England, Scotland, Wales and Northern Ireland.

It is important to realise that the Act does not only apply to divorced couples but applies to all parents, married or unmarried.

Under the Child Support Act, child support maintenance is an amount of money that an absent parent pays as a contribution to the upkeep of their children. The amount is worked out by taking account of each parent's income and essential outgoings. Both parents are treated in exactly the same way because each has an equal responsibility for the financial maintenance of their children. Maintenance will be reviewed every year and also following any change in either parent's circumstances.

WHO MUST APPLY FOR CHILD SUPPORT MAINTENANCE?

'Parents with care' is the term used to describe those parents who live with the children for whom maintenance is needed. 'Absent parents' is the term used to describe those parents who do not live with the children concerned.

The Child Support Agency will ask you about the absent parent. If you think that supplying this information will lead to problems, for example with regard to your safety, you can discuss with them how much you have to disclose.

People who are not the children's parents, but who have care of children whose parents live elsewhere can apply if they wish to do so.

Absent parents may also apply for a child support maintenance assessment to show the amount of maintenance that they should pay.

In addition, if a child of twelve or over is living in Scotland and at least one of the parents lives apart in England, Scotland, Wales or Northern Ireland, that child can apply direct to the Child Support Agency.

If you are a parent with care and get either Income Support, Family

Credit or Disability Working Allowance or you are the current partner of someone who gets one of these benefits then you must apply for assessment of child support maintenance if the Child Support Agency asks you to do so.

WHEN TO APPLY TO THE CHILD SUPPORT AGENCY

The Child Support Agency began to take on cases in stages from April 1993.

If you are a parent with care and you get Income Support, Family Credit or Disability Working Allowance, the Child Support Agency or benefits agency will write to you between April 1993 and March 1996 starting first with those people who are already receiving maintenance.

Parents with care who apply for the above benefits will be asked to apply for child support maintenance at the same time. Those whose Family Credit or Disability Working Allowance has been renewed since April 1993 will have been asked to apply for child support maintenance at the time of renewal of their Benefits.

If you are a parent with care and you do not get Income Support, Family Credit or Disability Working Allowance, and you do not have an existing child maintenance agreement (a court order, voluntary agreement maintenance agreement or minute of agreement) you may apply to the Child Support Agency straightaway . If you already have an existing child maintenance agreement you will be able to apply to the agency after April 1996.

If you are an absent parent and you do not have an existing child maintenance agreement you may apply to the Child Support Agency straightaway. If you already have an agreement you can apply after April 1996.

If you are a child over twelve who lives in Scotland, if the parent from whom you want to get child support maintenance does not pay child maintenance for you now, you may apply to the Child Support Agency straightaway. If child maintenance is already paid for you, you will be able to apply after April 1996.

HOW IS CHILD SUPPORT MAINTENANCE WORKED OUT?

The method used to work out the amount of child support maintenance will take into account the following:

- the day-to-day costs of maintaining a child;
- the income of the parent with care and the absent parent after making allowance for tax, national insurance and essential expenses, including rent or mortgage costs;
- any other children either parent may have.

There are safeguards to ensure that absent parents paying child support maintenance will have sufficient income to live on.

New partners of either parent will not be expected to pay anything towards the child support maintenance of children who are not their own.

If your child spends part of the time with one parent and part with another, the child support maintenance will be shared, provided that the child spends an average of two nights a week with the absent parent.

When making an application for maintenance, the parent with care will be asked to provide information about the absent parent. This helps the agency to locate this person.

If the parent with care does not know where the parent is then the Child Support Agency will try to find out through its own enquiries. If the absent parent cannot be contacted, no assessment for child support maintenance can be made. This can, however, be done at a later stage if the absent parent or his whereabouts can be traced.

IF AN ABSENT PARENT DOES NOT PAY . . .

If an absent parent does not pay, the parent with care may ask the Child Support Agency to ensure that payment is made. Payments to be made through the Agency will be followed up two days after being due.

Absent parents or parents with care whose circumstances have changed can, of course, ask for a new assessment. If, however, an absent parent does not have an acceptable reason for not paying, the Agency is likely to take one of a number of measures. These include making an order for payments to be deducted directly from wages or salary.

WHAT DOES THE ABSENT PARENT RECEIVING INCOME SUPPORT PAY?

If you are an absent parent getting Income Support and you are over eighteen, fit for work and have no dependent children living with you, then you may be required to make a contribution to the maintenance of your children of £2.20 per week.

If you do not receive Income Support or other Benefits the Child Support Agency will make an assessment of your income and outgoings to reach a level of support payable by you.

SERVICES OFFERED BY THE CHILD SUPPORT AGENCY

There are two services available:

- an assessment and review service where the Agency will make an assessment for child support maintenance and will review it each year;
- assessment review and collection service, where the agency provides a collection service in addition to assessment and review. The Agency may be asked to collect payments from the absent parent and pass them on to the parent with care.

Charges for the Agency's Services

The current standard annual fee for the assessment and review service is £44, which both parents will be asked to pay unless:

- they or their current partner get Income Support, Family Credit or

Disability Working Allowance;
- they are under sixteen, or under nineteen and in full-time education up to 'A' level standard or equivalent;
- their income falls below certain limits.

The standard annual fee for the collection service is £34, and both parents will be expected to pay this when either parent opts for the Agency's collection service. It is also payable by absent parents when the parent with care gets Income Support, Family Credit or Disability Working Allowance. Again, you may be exempt from payment if you are one of the groups referred to above.

The Child Support Agency will calculate the amount of child support maintenance using a formula agreed by Parliament. The formula is related to the requirements of each child in a family and the calculation is made for each parent if they have income other than Income Support.

FIVE STEPS TO THE WORKING OUT OF CHILD SUPPORT MAINTENANCE

A Work out the *basic maintenance requirement* for each child

B Work out the *net income* of each parent

C Work out the *essential expenditure* (known as 'exempt income') of each parent

D Calculate the *assessable income* of each parent (which is the sum available to pay maintenance out of) by subtracting essential expenditure from net income

E Calculate *child support maintenance* payable by setting assessable income against basic maintenance requirement using the formula agreed by Parliament

The following working example shows what is involved in calculating the weekly amount of child support maintenance payable and enables you to arrive at an indication of what might apply in your case. This is based on Child Support Rules currently in operation but it is a guideline only and if you require up to date figures you should contact the Child Support Agency on the number given on the last page of this chapter.

A Work out *basic maintenance requirement*

1. Write down one personal allowance for each child for whom child support maintenance is payable.

		Amount for my children
Child's personal allowance		
Child under 11	£15.05	_____
Child aged 11-15	£22.15	_____
Child aged 16-17	£26.45 *	_____
Child aged 18	£34.80 *	_____

* if in full time education up to 'A' level
or equivalent (children in higher education
are not included)

2. Include £9.65 for family expenses   _____

3 If they live with a parent who has not
   got a partner, add £4.90   _____

4 If at least one of the children above
   is under 16, add £44.90   _____

5 Add these figures together   _____

6 Take away the amount of child benefit
   received for the children. This is usually

£10 for the first child, and £8.10
for each other child   _____

Weekly *basic maintenance requirement*   _____

B Work out *net income*

Parents who get Income Support

There is no need to calculate the income of parents who get Income Support, or who are the partner of someone who is getting Income Support, for the purposes of child support maintenance.

If the absent parent gets Income Support there is no need to do the following calculation for either parent.

If the absent parent does not get Income Support you need to work out how much each parent should pay towards child support.

Parents with care of the children who get Income Support are counted as having no income for the purposes of child support maintenance assessment and there is no need to work out their income in the following calculation.

Net income is income after tax and National Insurance have been paid, and half of any superannuation or pension contributions.

1. Write down earnings from employment or self-employment, using a weekly average. If your earnings or the other parent's earnings vary, average them out over several weeks to give a weekly figure.

2. Add the weekly amount of any Family Credit, Invalidity Benefit, retirement pension, Statutory Sick Pay, or Disability Working Allowance Benefits and other Benefits, except the following:
   - Attendance Allowance
   - Disability Living Allowance
   - £10 a week of any war disablement or widows pension
   - Child Benefit

   These four are ignored completely for the purposes of calculating child maintenance.

3. Add the actual income you and/or the other parent get from capital such as bank or building society interest, or rents from properties, or from other sources. Work these out as a weekly amount.

4. Add in any other sort of income you receive, again worked out as a weekly amount.

The total of all these amounts makes up your weekly *net income*. Earnings and income from capital received by your present partner do not count as income for this calculation.

To help you work out your net income, use the following guide:

	you	other parent
Earnings after tax, national insurance and half of pension or superannuation contributions	____	____
plus		
Income from Benefits	____	____
Income from capital/investments	____	____
plus		
Any other income	____	____
net income	____	____

Absent parents who do not have other children of their own living with them will usually be expected to pay between 15-30% of this net income figure in child support maintenance, depending on their individual circumstances. Those with other children, or with a low income, will usually pay a smaller proportion of their net income in child support maintenance. The following information may help you to work out the amount payable in your case.

C Work out *essential expenditure*

The essential weekly expenditure of both parents is taken into account.

Write down the following amounts for each parent in the relevant column.

	you	other parent
A personal allowance for the adult of £44.00	_____	_____

An allowance for any
children of either parent
who live with them (including
children of a new marriage
or other relationships)   _____ _____
£15.05 for children under 11   _____ _____
£22.15 for child 11-15   _____ _____
£26.45 for child 16-17*   _____ _____
£34.80 for child 18*   _____ _____

* if in full time education
up to 'A' level standard or
equivalent (children in
higher education are excluded)
If you have included such a child
add £9.65 for family expenses _____ _____

If either parent is a lone
parent (that is, they have
not remarried or are not
now living with a partner)
add in the figure of £4.90   _____ _____

Then add in your weekly
housing costs and those
of any children of your
own who live with you. Do
the same for the other
parent (see note below)   _____   _____

Essential expenditure for each parent
'exempt income'   _____   _____

Note on housing costs: you are allowed your share of reasonable
weekly costs for housing, including any mortgage payment you make.
If you receive housing benefit, deduct this figure from your rent before
you add a figure for rent.

If you have remarried or now have a partner, and they, and/or their
stepchildren from a previous relationship, are living with you, the
housing costs you should add in here will be less than the full amount
your household pays. As a rough guide, if you have a partner, deduct a
quarter of the rent payment for them, and if there are children who are
not your natural or adopted children also living with you deduct a fifth
for each stepchild.

For example:

Your rent is   £40 per week
Your partner's   £10 a week
(25% of total)
Leaving   £30 a week

Add £30 for weekly housing costs in calculation above

Extra amounts are added to essential expenses if the parents or
children have disabilities. Ring the Child Support Agency for further
information.

D Calculate *assessable income*

The next step is to take the essential expenditure total away from the figure arrived for net income.

	you	other parent
Net income (part B)	_____	_____
Less essential expenditure allowance (part C)	_____	_____
Leaves total income a week of	_____	_____

The figure you now have is called the ***assessable income***. Child support maintenance is paid out of this income.

E Calculate *child support maintenance*

If you are an absent parent you are asked to pay 50 pence in every pound of your assessable income until the basic maintenance requirement is met. For example, if you worked out that the basic maintenance requirement for your children was £75, you would need £150 assessable income to pay this in full. This is because you pay 50p in each £1 assessable income in maintenance, and keep the other 50p for yourself.

You should note, however, that if the parent with care of the children also has an assessable income, this may reduce the amount the absent parent pays (see notes following).

Looking at another example, if the maintenance requirement for your children is £75 and your assessable income is £100, the most you will be required to pay will be £50 towards the maintenance costs (50p in every £1 of the £100, keeping the other 50p for yourself).

If paying this amount would make you worse off than you would be if you were on Income Support, you will be asked to pay a lower amount of child support maintenance. It is possible to tell you the full extent of this reduction only after you have made an application for maintenance assessment.

If, after you have paid for the basic maintenance requirement, you still have money left in your assessable income, then you are asked to carry on paying, but at the rate of 25p in the £1.

If the parent with care has assessable income too, this may reduce the amount the absent parent pays. If you and the other parent both have assessable income, add the two amounts together.

Your assessable income
plus _____
The other parent's assessable income _____
adds up to
Total joint assessable income _____

If the total joint assessable income figure you have just worked out is less than twice the amount of basic maintenance requirement, the absent parent pays whatever the calculation so far says the absent parent can afford.

If the total joint assessable income figure is more than twice the amount of the basic maintenance requirement, you need to work out what the proportion of the total is. For example, if you are the absent parent and your assessable income is £120, and the parent with care's assessable income is £80, your share of the £200 is six tenths (£120 ÷ £200). So you are responsible for paying six tenths of the maintenance requirement at the rate of 50p in the £1.

If you have assessable income left after paying your share of the basic maintenance requirement, you will continue to pay at the rate of 25p in each £1.

There is a maximum level of child maintenance above which the powers of the Child Support Agency cease. After that it will be up to each parent to ask the court to order an extra amount to be paid. The minimum amount is payable is £2.20.

CONTACTING THE CHILD SUPPORT AGENCY

If you need further advice or you require an application form from the Child Support Agency You should call:

THE CHILD SUPPORT AGENCY ENQUIRY LINE
0345 133 133.

This line is open between 9 a.m. to 6 p.m. on weekdays. Calls are charged at the local rate.

Alternatively you can write to the Child Support Agency at the following address:

Child Support Agency
PO Box 55
Brierley Hill
West Midlands
DY5 1YL

Please note: the contents of this chapter are current at time of going to press. If, however, you are thinking of applying for child support, you should contact the Child Support Agency. The information in this book is simply to give you an idea of the principles involved in working out financial support for children.

Now please read the KEY POINTS from chapter 6 opposite.

KEY POINTS

- The Child Support Act 1991, which came into force in April 1993, regulates the payments for the upkeep of children following divorce.

- The Child Support Agency assesses maintenance payments and the courts no longer decide on questions of financial provision for children unless payments exceed the amounts assessed by the Agency or there are special grounds such as educational needs.

- The courts still have jurisdiction to make orders for stepchildren and other children of the family. The courts will also still make lump sum orders and property adjustment orders for children. They will still also deal with disabled children.

- The Child Support Agency sets the framework within which questions such as who applies for maintenance, and when to apply, can be answered.

7

FINANCIAL ARRANGEMENTS

FAMILY ASSETS

When a marriage breaks down, everything which has been earned or owned during the marriage is considered part of the assets of that marriage. On divorce these assets can all be redistributed no matter who earned them during the marriage period. As the emphasis is on family assets, property owned by either spouse before the marriage cannot be counted.

If one spouse buys a house, however, or acquires some other asset, before marrying, with a view to living in it or using it together, this will be counted as an asset. When a divorce takes place, the couple concerned will usually decide between them what should happen to family assets, the most significant usually being the house, unless there is a large sum of money involved.

If an agreement cannot be reached concerning the division of assets then the couple can ask the court to decide who is to have what. The court has very wide powers to redistribute the family assets. Its task is to try to reach a fair and just division in all the circumstances of each case.

The duty of husband and wife to support each other does not end on divorce. In principle, the duty to maintain remains. In particular, the court must consider whether it would not be desirable to impose a clean break on the couple. This is seen as an alternative to long-term support. It is obligatory for the courts to consider the question of ending one spouses financial dependence on the other, once the marriage itself has come to an end.

The main difficulty in making a judgement of this kind is that circumstances will vary so much from one couple to another. The main guidelines for the court are:

* to consider how long the couple have been married;
* to consider how old the parties to the marriage are;
* to consider whether there are any children involved.

If a marriage has been short lived, the parties to it are young and there are no children involved then the courts would almost certainly want to see a clean break.

THE ONE–THIRD RULE

In general, if a clean break from marriage is not ordered, the court calculates on the basis of the 'one third' rule. Using this formula the wife gets one third of the combined income – exclusive of maintenance for the children. This is not a rigid rule but the basis for starting calculations in each case.

FACTORS WHICH ARE TAKEN INTO ACCOUNT BY THE COURT WHEN MAKING AN ORDER

The court will look at the income of each partner, earning capacity, property and other financial resources. This amounts, usually, to the total family resources and is what the court will look at beyond what is said by the parties.

Other matters taken into account by a court would be expectations under a will or other family settlement.

The court will also look at financial needs, obligations and responsibilities, both now and in the near future. This covers all outgoings such as food, clothing and other essential items. If either spouse has set up home with another partner or intends to remarry, then that second family's needs will also be an important factor in the equation.

Parties to a marriage are not expected to be in the position that they would have been in if the marriage had survived. Nevertheless, in the case of very wealthy households, adjustments are sometimes made to compensate for loss of standards.

A court will take into account how old parties to a marriage are. A younger person may need less support than an elderly one. If either spouse suffers from a disability or serious illness, this will obviously be a factor in assessing the division of assets.

PENSION RIGHTS

The question of pension rights, following divorce is fraught with problems and is currently under scrutiny. Pensions almost always represent a considerable aspect of family investment in the long term. For a couple who divorce late in life, the loss of pension rights can mean a considerable loss of future material comfort.

A woman can also lose the prospect of a widow's pension once she is divorced.

In May 1993, a court allowed a wife a share of her husband's pension on divorce. Legislation, however, will have to deal with the whole question of pension rights on divorce and a decision is expected shortly.

PROTECTION OF ASSETS

If there is manoeuvring before the divorce is finalised, for example one spouse attempting to engineer the division of assets to his or her favour, then there is a series of steps which a divorcing spouse should be aware of which can prevent this happening.

THE HOME

This is usually the most significant asset at stake and it is essential to ensure that this is not sold or otherwise disposed of without your knowledge.

If your name is on the title deeds of the property then it cannot be sold without your knowledge or consent. However, if you are uncertain of this, it is essential that you consult a solicitor and ensure that you can register a land charge or notice on the property. This notice would ensure that any would-be purchaser is fully aware of your right to live in the property. If the property was sold then the person buying would be obliged to let you continue living there.

PROTECTION FROM THE COURTS GENERALLY

If you can satisfy the courts that you have a claim to a share of the family assets or income and that your spouse is about to make off with some of your assets, or already has done so, the court can prevent this taking place.

If you are seriously worried that this will be the case then you should contact your solicitor immediately. It is easier to act before anything takes place than afterwards.

A court can make an injunction to prevent your spouse from disposing of any of the family assets. If he or she does not obey this injunction then imprisonment can follow. The court could also make an order that your spouse pay over money to an independent person for safe keeping, such as a court account or bank account.

If you find out that your spouse has got rid of assets after the event, the process of reclaiming is that much harder. The court has the power to set transactions aside, only provided that they were not made with someone who has paid a proper price and was ignorant of the circumstances.

An example could be shares in a company. If the disposal was to general purchasers, then the ability of the court to get back those stocks is very limited. However, if another party was involved, such as a relative, and the disposal, to that person, was in full knowledge of the circumstances then the court's job is that much easier

OBTAINING FINANCIAL HELP BEFORE DIVORCE IS FINALISED

In the early stages of the divorce, you will usually have to rely on your own savings or earnings until a settlement can be reached. Usually, it is the woman who is hardest hit and this section will assume that it is the woman who is seeking help.

Sooner or later, however, you will need more concrete assistance and there are two ways of obtaining this: by applying to the court for an order obliging your husband to maintain you and by applying for welfare benefits.

STATE AND OTHER BENEFITS

There are various Benefits available. There is a booklet, at the time of writing, called 'Which Benefit'which can be obtained from your local social security office. This booklet gives up-to-date information on the type of Benefits currently available and your eligibility.

There are a number of other leaflets available from other sources. The Child Poverty Action Group, for example, publish several guides and a regular information bulletin about Benefits.

None of the Benefits are dependent on National Insurance contributions. The Benefit levels assume that you are separated. If you have not yet separated, you will have general difficulty obtaining Benefits because of the assumed continuing support of your partner.

If you are in financial difficulty whilst still living with your spouse you should seek advice about entitlement to Benefits from a Citizens' Advice Bureau or from your local social security office. There are circumstances, for example, where you can arrange to have your husband's Income Support paid to you instead of him, if he is refusing to support you and the children properly.

TYPE OF HELP AVAILABLE ONCE DIVORCE PROCEEDINGS HAVE COMMENCED

The divorce court can order a spouse to make regular cash payments to another to provide for needs until the divorce comes through. This is known as 'maintenance pending suit', or maintenance until the divorce is decided.

The court cannot order a spouse to make more substantial payments or divide assets until divorce has been granted. The court can, however, make an order as to who lives in the house until divorce, if the breakdown means that you cannot live under the same roof together.

The court can also take steps to prevent either of you from disposing of any of your property before it has taken the opportunity to consider what should be done with it in the future, if it feels that the disposal will affect future equal and fair distribution.

You can apply for a court order at any stage between the commencement of proceedings and the date on which decree nisi of divorce is made absolute, whether or not you are living apart.

If an order is made – maintenance pending suit – this will tide you over until longer-term plans can be made. Maintenance pending suit therefore ceases to be payable when your divorce is made absolute.

If when your divorce has been finalised an order still has not been made, a maintenance pending suit order can be replaced by an 'interim periodical order' which lasts until a final order is made.

When looking at the circumstances of your case in order to be able to make a maintenance pending suit order, the judge will look at the circumstances of both parties and concentrate on achieving a fair balance between what you need and what your spouse can pay.

You will both be expected to provide details of your income from all sources and your regular expenses. Assessing your income and expenses may not always be that straightforward. For example, Social Security Benefits may vary depending on whether or not you receive maintenance.

You may have formed a relationship with another person. The fact that you have committed adultery will not normally prevent you receiving maintenance from your spouse. However, if you are living with another person, that person will probably help you to pay for your everyday needs. If this is the case, then maintenance will be reduced.

A good guide to whether or not you are entitled to maintenance pending suit is to draw up a chart which indicates whether or not your income exceeds your outgoings. If you earn more than you spend you are unlikely to get maintenance.

If neither of you have commenced divorce proceedings, you will not be able to apply for maintenance. There are, however, other ways in which you can obtain assistance from the courts. The magistrates' court can, for example, make various orders to provide maintenance.

The first requirement for an order like this is to demonstrate that you are eligible for such an order.

IF YOU HAVE NOT YET COMMENCED DIVORCE PROCEEDINGS...

If you have not yet commenced divorce proceedings, you will not be able to apply to the divorce court for maintenance pending suit. However, there are other ways in which you can obtain assistance from the courts.

THE MAGISTRATES' COURT

In order to obtain help with your financial situation from a magistrates' court, you must be able to show that you are eligible for a magistrates' court order. The following sets out the ways in which you can qualify for an order and the type of order that can be made.

If you can prove that:

- your husband has deserted you;
- your husband has behaved unreasonably;
- your husband has failed to provide reasonable maintenance for you;

- your husband has failed to provide or make reasonable contribution towards the maintenance of a child of the family;

you can expect to obtain an order for maintenance payable to you at regular intervals and/or a lump sum payment of not more than £1000.

If you and your husband have come to a financial arrangement that you would both like the court to put into an order, the court can grant maintenance on the basis of what you have agreed between you.

If you and your husband have been separated by agreement for more than three months and your husband has been making maintenance payments to you and you would like the additional security of an order, a court can grant this order, subject to certain restrictions.

Magistrates will decide on a sum to be paid by taking into account your needs and how much your husband can afford to pay.

If you are still living together . . .

If you are living together when you apply to the magistrates' court, you can still obtain an order from the court. If you go on living together for a continuous period of more than six months after the order is made, an order for maintenance will cease to be effective.

If you are living apart when you get an order, but you subsequently start to live together again, your maintenance order will cease if you live together for a continuous period of more than six months.

Now please read the KEY POINTS from chapter 7 opposite.

KEY POINTS

- When a marriage breaks down, everything which has been owned during the marriage is considered part of the assets of that marriage.

- If an agreement cannot be reached concerning the division of assets, the couple can ask the court to decide who is to have what. The court has very wide powers to redistribute family assets.

- In general, if a 'clean break' from marriage is not ordered, the court will calculate division of assets using the 'one-third rule', that is one-third to a given partner.

- The court will look at the income of each partner: earning capacity; property; and other financial resources, before making an order. The court will also look at financial needs and obligations.

- There are various benefits available once you are divorced or separated. Advice and literature can be obtained from a number of agencies, that is, the Department of Social Security, the Child Poverty Action Group and Citizens' Advice Bureaux.

- Whilst you are separated, the divorce county court can make an order for 'maintenance pending suit' or maintenance until the divorce has been decided.

- The magistrates' court can also make orders, if you have not yet applied for a divorce.

8

LONGER-TERM FINANCIAL ARRANGEMENTS

Questions concerning your house, the sharing out of other assets and your future income will all loom large when you realise that you are to be divorced.

If you and your spouse can reach agreement about these questions then obviously the whole process will be easier. If you cannot agree as to what should happen, you can ask the court to decide for you and grant an order.

It is usually the job of a district judge of the divorce court to consider your case and formulate future arrangements for you. The final order made by the district judge, usually called an 'ancillary relief order', will be specific to your circumstances.

THE ORDERS THAT A COURT CAN MAKE

The court has wide powers to adjust your rights to property and income after the divorce to make sure that proper provision is made for the whole family. The range of potential orders comprises two categories:

1. orders concerned with income and with the payment of lump sums of money;
2. orders concerned with the families capital assets, often referred to as

'property adjustment orders'.

1. Financial provision orders

For husband and wife there are three types of financial provision order that the court can make:

a) An order for periodical payments. This is commonly known as a 'maintenance order'. It obliges one spouse to pay the other a sum of money at regular intervals, usually every week or every month. The payment will normally go towards living expenses. An order for periodical payments will end automatically on the death or remarriage of the recipient or on the death of the payer.

b) An order for secure periodical payments. This is an order for maintenance coupled with an order that the payer of the maintenance should guarantee the payments in some way, such as setting aside assets that will provide sufficient income to cover the maintenance ordered. It will end automatically if the recipient dies or remarries but it will not necessarily end on the death of the payer. The courts do not often make orders for secure periodical payments unless the family concerned is fairly wealthy.

c) A lump sum order. This is an order whereby one spouse is ordered to pay the other a substantial sum of money. It is different from the payment of maintenance because it is generally a 'once and for all' payment whereas maintenance imposes a continuous obligation to pay at regular intervals over a period of time.

Maintenance for children

The responsibility for fixing maintenance for children will now normally be that of the Child Support Agency rather than the courts although the courts still have a limited power to make orders for maintenance for children which will usually only be exercised in the case of rather better off families or where there is a disabled child.

The courts have power to make lump sum payments in favour of children. This power can normally only be used in relation to children who are under eighteen but older children can benefit if they are still being educated or trained, or where there are special circumstances.

2. Property adjustment orders

For husband and wife the court's powers are very far reaching indeed. If it so wishes the court can reallocate all of your property between you in the way that it sees fit. It can, for example, order one of you to transfer property that you own to the other or to share it with your spouse or to settle it on trust for your spouse or to sell it and divide the proceeds between you.

For the children the court can even allocate some of your property to your children if this seems appropriate. However, most families cannot afford to benefit the children directly in this way as they need all their assets to provide for themselves and their children after the divorce. The court therefore will only contemplate transferring some of your assets to your children if you are well off.

The court can, of course, combine several orders in one case. It is common, therefore, to find that the court makes an order in relation to the matrimonial home and orders one spouse to pay maintenance to the other spouse.

HOW THE COURT APPROACHES THE PROBLEM

The court will need details of assets and earnings you have between you and what you are both going to need for the future by way of capital and income.

You might find it helpful, in the initial stages, to draw up a balance sheet listing your joint assets and requirements. This will help both you and the court. You should list capital assets such as your house, whether you own or rent it, your furniture, insurance policies, etc. You should also list income which will probably be mainly derived from your employment but also could be from investments.

Try to put a value on your capital assets. Your house should be valued, probably by an estate agent. You should also determine the value of outstanding loans and mortgages. In addition , you should work out how easily realisable your assets are.

When you ask the court to determine what should happen to your family assets and income after your divorce the court has a free hand to do whatever is fair and practical. Instead of being the only consideration, the question of ownership becomes merely one of the many factors that the court can take into account in reaching its decision.

The law provides that in deciding on the orders it should make, the court should give first consideration to the welfare of any children of the family who are under eighteen but also must take into account all the circumstances of the case.

In the case of provision for a husband or wife, these circumstances include:

a) the income, earning capacity, property and other financial resources which each of you has or is likely to have in the foreseeable future;
b) the financial needs, obligations and responsibilities that each of you has or is likely to have in the foreseeable future;
c) the standard of living that you enjoyed as a family before the breakdown of your marriage;
d) how old you both are and how long the marriage has lasted;
e) any physical or mental disabilities you may have;
f) the contributions that you have both made or are likely to make in the foreseeable future to the welfare of the family;
g) whether either of you will lose the chance of acquiring any benefit as a result of divorce;
h) in some cases, the conduct of each of you.

Remarriage is not one of the circumstances that the court is specifically directed to take into account. Nonetheless, it can be relevant to the court's decision. You should see chapter 9 on the effects of this.

When considering what provision to make for your children, the court is directed to consider very similar factors, for example, what the child needs, what resources it has (if any), whether there are any disabilities, etc. It can also consider whether you and your spouse had intended the child to be educated and trained, so if for example you had originally intended the child to go to a fee-paying school, the court will try to come to an arrangement that will enable the parent with residence to go ahead with the plan.

Some of the factors mentioned above need an explanation.

INCOME AND EARNING CAPACITY

The court will look at the income of each of you before and after tax, taking into account the expenses that you incur, such as National Insurance contributions. If you are employed, your income will be apparent from your past pay slips. If you are self-employed, the court will look at previous years accounts. If you receive state benefits that are not means tested, these will be taken into account. Benefits that depend on your means, such as income support, will generally be ignored because they will be affected by whatever order the court makes.

PERKS

Some employees receive perks from their employers, for instance, the use of a company car, luncheon vouchers, etc. The court will usually take this kind of advantage into account.

UNEMPLOYED SPOUSE

If one partner is unemployed, and in this case we usually refer to the male, the court will not make an order that he would only be able to afford to pay from regular earnings. On the other hand, if he is voluntarily out of work and there is employment available to him if he chooses to take it, the court might decide to put pressure on him to go back to work by, say, making a maintenance order that he could only afford to pay if he had a regular wage.

If the wife is unemployed, it is within the court's power to decide that a wife should receive reduced or no maintenance for a limited period only, because she should be working. However, the court would never take this action unless it is very clear that there are jobs available for her.

If employment is available for the wife, the court will not penalise her for not taking it until it has gone into all the circumstances. It will look at your past arrangements about work. If, with the husband's agreement, the wife has never worked during the marriage, the court will not necessarily ask her to go out and get a job because she is divorced. On the other hand, if she has got a job she will not be able to give it up and rely on her husband to support her after divorce. If she is young, with no children and can get a job then she will be expected to do so to relieve the husband of responsibility for her.

If there are children to look after, this will obviously affect the wife's ability to work. It is generally accepted that the wife is entitled to stay at home to look after young children unless of course, she has previously been accustomed to working and bringing up the family, during the marriage. This may mean that she cannot work at all, or that she can only be expected to do a part-time job.

If either spouse remarries or starts to live with a new partner, this will obviously affect your financial position for better or worse. The court will not give your former spouse a share in the income or assets of the new partner. However, if your new partner pools his or her resources with you, you may find that you have more income and assets available to maintain your former spouse and children. This will be taken into account.

NEEDS AND OBLIGATIONS

1. A home. Both of you will probably need a home for yourself and children. The court will concentrate very much on making sure that everyone has a roof over their head for the future.
2. Mortgages and loans. In making arrangements for your future you

may well run into debt. If you have had to borrow money for reasonable purposes the court will take account of the fact that you will have to repay this sum for interest.

3. Obligations to a new partner. Far from providing you with additional resources, your new partner may well be a drain on your income. You may need to provide him or her with a new home. The court will take this into account when assessing your position but will look upon your obligations to your former family as equally important.

4. Ensuring that you both have enough income for your needs. Where a couple have a very low income between them, the court will have to concentrate particularly on providing for their essential needs. The court will make sure that, if it orders one spouse to maintain the other, this will not reduce that spouse's income for his own needs below subsistence level. If this means that he cannot be ordered to pay the other spouse sufficient for her needs, she will have to rely on state benefits to make up the shortfall.

HOW LONG THE MARRIAGE HAS LASTED

Obviously a wife with no children who has been married for only a short time has less right to call on her husband for continuing maintenance and a share in his capital assets than a wife who has been married for some years and has brought up or is bringing up children. A young wife with no children after a short marriage can often only expect to get out of the marriage the equivalent of what she put into it. In other words, she will be entitled to a share in the capital assets only if she contributed to them financially or by her own efforts.

YOUR CONTRIBUTIONS TO THE WELFARE OF THE FAMILY

Many couples make equal contributions to family life, although in different ways. Often the wife makes her contribution by caring for the family and the husband makes his by working and contributing financially. In some cases however, one spouse makes a greater contribution than the other. In such a situation, it may well be fair for that spouse to take a larger share of the family assets when the marriage breaks down.

THE CONDUCT OF BOTH OF YOU

When a marriage breaks down, a fair share of the blame usually attaches to both parties. So in most cases, the way in which you have behaved will not affect a court's decision on your property or maintenance. However, there are two situations in which conduct can affect a court's order:

1. If either of you has behaved so badly that most ordinary people would feel that he or she should not receive as much income or property as usual, the court can adjust its order appropriately.
2. If you start to live with someone else who supports you, this will be taken into account in assessing what orders should be made in your favour. And, of course if you actually remarry, you will automatically lose your right to maintenance for yourself.

COPING WITH PARTICULAR PROBLEMS

The house

When it comes to dealing with the matrimonial home, the court will attempt to arrive at an arrangement that ensures that both of you and particularly the children, have a home, whilst still rewarding you fairly for the contributions that you have made to the marriage generally and to the acquisition of the house and other assets in particular.

This is not always possible. One spouse (usually the one who is looking after the children) may therefore come away from the marriage with more capital than seems strictly fair in relation to his or her contribution because this is the only way to ensure that he or she is able to get somewhere to live after the divorce.

Generally, if you are accustomed to owning your own house or to be buying it on a mortgage, the court will try to devise an arrangement for the future that will enable both of you to continue as an owner-occupier. However, this cannot always be done and as a last resort, the court may have to come down in favour of an arrangement that provides one of you (normally the spouse looking after the children) with a home of your own and obliges the other to rely on rented accommodation, at least for the time being.

The court usually has a number of options in relation to the house. There are two sorts of arrangements possible – those that involve the sale of the house and those that enable one of you to continue living in the house. The following are the more common alternatives open to the court:

- The court can order that the house be sold at once and the proceeds be divided between you as it thinks fair. This is really only practicable when the proceeds of sale will be sufficiently large to enable both of you to obtain alternative accommodation. If either of you will be able to obtain a mortgage to assist in such a purchase, the court can take this into account. However, this will not always be possible particularly for a wife who is entirely dependent on maintenance.

- The court can order that the house should be sold but postpone the sale to some time in the future. This used to be done quite frequently where one spouse was looking after the children and needed to go on living in the house to provide them with a home. The court used to postpone the sale until the youngest child reached seventeen or eighteen. Nowadays, this type of order is looked upon less favourably by the courts because it is artificial to treat family life as ending when the children reach seventeen or eighteen – many children live with their parents, at least in holidays from college or university, for some time after their seventeenth or eighteenth birthdays.

- The court can order that the house be allocated to one of you but give the other the right to part of the proceeds of sale when the house is sold. This normally means that one of you has all the rights of an owner over the house and can decide when and if to sell it, but the other is deprived of both his home and capital asset at least for the time being. Before it makes an order of this kind therefore, the court will want to make sure that whoever does not have the house can get somewhere else to live.

- The court can allocate the house to one of you and order that spouse to pay the other a lump sum forthwith in compensation. Whether this is feasible will depend on how much the spouse with the house can raise (a loan or mortgage may present insuperable problems for a spouse dependent on maintenance) and how much, if anything, the other spouse needs to purchase alternative accommodation.

- The court can allocate the house to one spouse and compensate the other spouse by, for example, relieving him or her of the obligation to pay any maintenance for the spouse who receives the house.

Rented accommodation

If you rent your home from the council or housing association, or private landlord, the court can generally allocate the tenancy to one of you, irrespective of whose name it is in. It would be most likely to do this in favour of the spouse who has the custody of the children.

The contents of the house and other assets

You will find the court reluctant to get involved in disputes between you over routine items of furniture and furnishings. You will be expected to sort this out amongst yourselves. People often find it more convenient for the spouse left in the matrimonial home to take the contents of the house, while the other receives some other form of compensation.

If you fail to agree and you ask the court to sort things out for you, you may well find that it simply orders that the whole lot be sold and the proceeds divided between you.

Valuable assets

Valuable assets such as savings, antiques, stocks and shares will usually be distributed by you in as equitable a fashion as possible. If not, the court will divide them in whatever way seems fair bearing in mind your needs and the way in which the assets were originally acquired.

Business

If one of you owns a business, that is, strictly speaking, property the court can reallocate between you on divorce. In practice, the court is unlikely to make any order that will damage your business interests or force you to sell up. Nor will you be required to take your spouse into partnership with you.

However, if your spouse has helped you to build up your business (for example, by serving in your shop, or by doing the books, or helping in your hotel, or by simply staying at home and looking after the domestic arrangements whilst you run the business) he or she will be entitled to have the value of this help reflected in the share he or she gets in the other family assets.

Pensions

Often one spouse (usually the husband) has made much better pension provision than the other during the marriage and the court has to do what it can to even things up between them. Although, at present the court's powers are limited, a recent court case has ruled that in one particular instance a wife should be allowed to share in the husband's pension on divorce. Further legislation is expected to equalise this situation and ensure that divorced women are not left without any pension rights on divorce.

Maintenance

Both husband and wife are entitled to apply for maintenance. However, by far the majority of claims are made by the wife and this section therefore deals with a wife's claim to maintenance. The same principles apply to a husband's claim.

The trend recently has been towards enabling a couple to achieve a clean break from each other whenever possible after divorce. If maintenance has to be paid from one to the other, a clean break will not be possible. The court is therefore likely to investigate the possibility of an arrangement that does not involve maintenance such as giving the wife a larger than average share of the family's capital assets so that she can be self-supporting.

Many couples are not in a position to make a clean break. If the court has to make a maintenance order, it will do so by giving careful consideration to your particular circumstances and its order will be tailored to your reasonable needs and your husband's ability to pay.

Now please read the KEY POINTS from chapter 8 opposite.

KEY POINTS

• The divorce courts will consider your case and formulate future financial arrangements for you. Orders fall into two categories, those concerned with income and the payment of lump sums of money, and those concerned with the family's capital assets, often referred to as 'property adjustment orders'.

• The court will take into account facts such as future earning power when making financial orders. They will also look at basic needs and obligations.

• In certain cases, the way one or other party has behaved during the breakdown of the marriage will affect the court's decision concerning property or maintenance in the future.

9

OTHER CONSIDERATIONS FOLLOWING DIVORCE

REMARRIAGE

You are only free to remarry when your divorce is made final by decree absolute. Before you are allowed to marry in any church or registry office, you will need to produce a copy of the decree absolute.

When you remarry, your entitlement to regular payments from your spouse will cease. This is not the case for children, who will continue to be entitled.

Orders that have already been made in relation to your property and capital will not, however, be affected by your remarriage.

If the spouse who has an obligation to make frequent payments remarries, this will not alter his liability to continue to make these payments. Liability can only be reduced or extinguished if it can be demonstrated that his or her circumstances have changed as a result of remarriage, which would affect ability to pay.

Once you have remarried, you are no longer entitled to begin a claim for property adjustment orders or for a lump sum payment. This is not the case if you have started the claim before you remarry, you will be allowed to continue with it. You should ensure that all necessary claims to property and other assets are in place before you remarry. Your solicitor will help you with this if necessary.

Your rights in relation to children will usually be totally unaffected by remarriage. However, in the unlikely event of your remarrying or someone totally unsuitable to be in contact with your children, you could find that your spouse will apply for an order depriving you of contact with them.

TAX AND YOUR DIVORCE

People are generally affected by three forms of tax during their lives – income tax, inheritance tax and capital gains tax.

Everyone knows what income tax is. Basically, it is the tax we pay from our earnings. However, inheritance tax is a little more complicated. This is the tax payable on your assets when you pass away and on any money or property you have transferred within seven years of your death. You will not normally need to involve yourself with inheritance tax at the time of divorce.

Capital gains tax is far more relevant to divorcing couples. This form of taxation is payable on capital gains that are made when you are disposing of property during your lifetime. The Inland Revenue treats property given away as 'disposed of'. This therefore attracts capital gains tax, or is treated as a capital gain.

Although you will be liable for capital gains tax when you dispose of property, you would not do so if you gave away money. This is exempt. There are also other exemptions from capital gains tax, for example you are permitted to make gains each year on property values, currently £5,800 per year (using tax year 1993/4 as a guide).

THE TAX POSITION WHEN LIVING TOGETHER AS A COUPLE

Income tax

Everyone is entitled to a tax free element within their income each year, known as the personal allowance. This amount will vary according to your circumstances, ie, whether you are married or single.

After 6th of April 1990, the system of joining husband and wife's income together for tax purposes ended and a new system was introduced. Now husband and wife are taxed separately on their earned and investment income. Each has a single person's allowance.

In addition to this, there is still a married couple's allowance which is normally set against a husbands income but can also be set against a woman's earnings. However, both of the partners can claim half of the allowance which will be split equally between them.

Capital gains tax is also no longer combined and a husband and wife will be taxed independently on his or her capital gains and will be entitled to a tax free allowance to set against them.

While you live together as husband and wife you can dispose of property to each other without incurring a capital gains tax. However, if the property is disposed of later to someone else then a capital gains tax is payable.

THE TAX POSITION ON LIVING APART

Separation will affect your tax position. For tax purposes, you are living apart if you are separated under a court order or a deed of separation or you are separated in such a way, or circumstance, that your separation is likely to be permanent.

The Inland Revenue imposes special rules during the year that you separate. Each person will have a single person's allowance and there will be a married couple's allowance which will be split as it was when you separated. If you have any of the children living with you who are under sixteen, or over sixteen and still undergoing further education at school, university or other college, you may be able to claim an additional personal allowance for the remainder of the year of separation but not if you are already receiving the full married couple's allowance.

After the end of the tax year in which you separate:

- You both continue to be taxed as individuals on your earned and unearned income. You will each be responsible to the Inland Revenue in respect of your own tax.
- Normally, you will both only get a single person's allowance.
- Either one or both of you may be able to claim the additional personal allowance if you are looking after one or more of the children.

Separated spouses are treated as single people for the purposes of capital gains tax. During the first year, or the tax year within which you separate, you can make tax free disposals to your spouse. After that ends, so does this right.

After divorce

Most of the tax changes experienced by yourself will happen when you cease to live together. The act of divorce only finalises these changes.

MAINTENANCE PAYMENTS AND INCOME TAX

In 1988, the treatment of maintenance payments, and the tax position was simplified. Although certain of the older orders and maintenance agreements remain under older rules, all other orders are subject to the new rules as set out below.

The payer

If the court orders that you make maintenance payments to a spouse, or ex-spouse either for his or her own benefit, or a child's benefit, or you enter into a legally binding agreement to do so, you should get tax relief on the payments.

You will get this tax relief through your PAYE code or tax assessment. Relief for your maintenance payments will continue if you remarry but will cease if your spouse remarries.

The recipient
The maintenance you receive will be tax free. This also applies to your children.

SHARING OUT PROPERTY AND CAPITAL GAINS TAX

Until you separate, and in the year of Separation, you can agree between you whatever re-allocation of assets you wish without any immediate liability to capital gains tax.

After you separate, and following the end of that particular tax year, gains that you make when transferring property to your spouse could be liable to capital gains tax depending on the type of property involved. As stated previously, you can share out savings but if you have to sell an item to pay off your spouse then you may be liable to pay tax.

When you dispose of your house to your spouse, or previous spouse, it is not always possible to escape entirely from capital gains tax. This is because any gain which is made when disposing of a property that was your main home is exempt from capital gains tax provided that you have been absent from it for more than three years and that no other house has replaced it as your residence, or main residence.

Even if you have moved out more than three years ago, you may still escape capital gains tax if you transfer an interest in the house to your spouse as part of a financial settlement on divorce or Separation, provided your spouse has continued to occupy the house as her only main home.

ENFORCING COURT ORDERS AND AGREEMENTS

Problems usually arise over payment of maintenance, in that they are sporadic or stop altogether. However, problems do also arise over arrangements for property. Courts can resolve problems such as these.

Maintenance problems
If you have come to a formal agreement with your spouse concerning payment of maintenance and your spouse fails to pay, the courts can

order him or her to pay as agreed. This is the same if the order has been made by the court and is broken The method of enforcement will depend on which court made the order.

Enforcement in the magistrates' court

If the court order has been registered in the magistrates' court because problems of future payments were foreseen, it is the responsibility of the magistrates' court to chase up non-payment.

Magistrates' courts can take several different views about non-payment. They can, for example, decide that your spouse should be excused from some or all arrears. This does not excuse your spouse from future liability.

The magistrates' court can also make arrangements for your spouse to pay off the arrears in instalments along with the current maintenance due.

An attachment of earnings order can also be made. It is addressed to the employer, if one exists, and directs the paying of frequent sums of money from the spouse's earnings.

The court can also order that your spouse be sent to prison for non-payment of maintenance. This is usually a last resort but is a frequent occurrence, as Her Majesty's Prisons will testify.

If you receive regular payments of income support, because of the low level of maintenance paid by your spouse, you may want to make over your maintenance order to the Department of Social Security. This means that the magistrates' court will pay over sums to the DSS instead of you. You will then be entitled to draw full income support, irrespective of what is paid to you by your spouse.

If your order has not been registered in the magistrates' court it will be up to you to request your spouse to reappear before the magistrates' court to get an order to pay. You should keep a clear and accurate record of payments made to you.

If your spouse goes abroad, the act of collecting unpaid maintenance becomes that much harder and you will need help from a solicitor in deciding a way forward.

Child support maintenance
If your case has been referred to the Child Support Agency, the Agency will automatically collect the child support maintenance for you if you are in receipt of State Benefits and will do so, on request, in other cases.

VARIATION OF AGREEMENTS IN THE FUTURE
The courts have powers to vary orders at a later date if circumstances change.

Maintenance orders
You are more likely to require a change in the divorce court's maintenance order than in any other court order. Although the court will vary orders, you have to put forward a good case for the change.

If you were awarded or ordered to pay a lump sum in one instalment, the court will not be able to alter this order on a subsequent occasion. If the lump sum is paid in more than one instalment then this can be altered.

If the court made an order in relation to your property on your divorce neither of you can ask for this order to be varied at a later date. However, if the court granted you 'liberty to apply' or ordered a sale on some of your property when it made the order, you can seek further assistance in putting the order into practice.

Child support maintenance
If you receive child support maintenance, the amount will automatically be reviewed by the Child Support Agency at regular intervals. Either parent has the right to apply to the Child Support Officer for review if the circumstances have changed and the maintenance assessment is likely to be substantially altered as a result.

IF YOU HAVE A WILL
It is usual for all your property and assets (estate) to pass to your marriage partner in the event of your death. However, on breakdown of

marriage it is usual for your will, if you have one, to be substantially altered.

If you die without making a will, this is known as dying intestate. If you die intestate before decree absolute of divorce is granted, as a general rule all your personal belongings will pass to your spouse, together with a large proportion of your money and your interests in land.

If you die intestate after the divorce is finalised, your spouse will have no automatic right to any of your estate. Your children would probably inherit the estate. However, provided your spouse has not remarried, he or she can make an application to the court for a share of the estate on the grounds that provision for his or her maintenance should have been made for after your death.

Changing your will

If you die after decree absolute has been granted leaving a will made before you were divorced, then unless it is clear that your intention is for the former spouse's position to be unaffected by the divorce, any clause leaving anything to him or her will automatically become ineffective, as will any appointment of him or her as your executor.

If you die before decree absolute your spouse will still be able to benefit from the will. It is advisable to produce a fresh will which takes into account your new circumstances following divorce and possible remarriage. You may want to consider making the new will effective from the date of the decree nisi in case you were to die in the intervening six weeks before the decree absolute is granted.

Surprisingly, the area of wills is one which is very neglected and which causes a lot of pain and anxiety following divorce and the death of one or other partner, so do make sure you give some thought to it.

Now please read the KEY POINTS from chapter 9 opposite.

KEY POINTS

- You are only free to remarry when your divorce is final by decree absolute.

- When you remarry, your entitlement to regular payments from your spouse will cease. This is not the case for children, who will continue to be entitled. Orders already made in relation to your property and capital will not be affected.

- Rights in relation to children will usually be totally unaffected by remarriage, with the exception of unsuitable remarriage.

- Although you will be liable for capital gains tax when you dispose of property, this is not the case with money transactions as these are free of capital gains tax.

- Separating will affect your tax position. For tax purposes, you are living apart if you are separated under a court order or deed of separation. After the end of the tax year in which you separate, you both continue to be taxed as individuals. Normally, you will only get a single person's allowance.

- Until you separate, in the year of separating, you can agree between you whatever reallocation of assets you wish without any immediate liability for capital gains tax.

- After you separate, and following the end of that tax year, you will be liable for capital gains tax.

- On the breakdown of your marriage, it is essential that you review your will, as inevitably your circumstances will have changed.

10

PROPOSED CHANGES TO THE DIVORCE LAW

The Government has put forward new proposals for the reform of the divorce laws. It believes that marriage needs to be more actively supported and that divorce law and procedures need reform.

* Marriage should receive more support
* Couples considering divorce should first consider the implications of divorce
* Allegations of fault should no longer be used
* There should be twelve months for reflection on whether the marriage can be saved
* Arrangements for children, finance and property should be decided before the divorce is granted
* Divorce should be barred where the dissolution of the marriage would cause grave financial or other grave hardship
* Family mediation should be introduced as part of the divorce process

Marriage should receive more support

The Government has stated that it wants to reinforce the importance of the institution of marriage. The Lord Chancellor has already taken over responsibility for funding marriage guidance organisations, and his Department is chairing an inter-departmental Working Group which is looking at ways to support people preparing for marriage and in marriage. This will include targeting available resources where need is greatest. The better people understand what marriage involves, the better they will be able to handle its ups and downs. The sooner they seek help when they are in difficulties, the more effectively they can be helped.

Couples considering divorce should first consider the implications of divorce

At present many couples get divorced very quickly, and they may not think about all the issues.

Under the new system, anyone seeking a divorce will have to go to an information session before starting the divorce process. This will give details of the separation and divorce process and the effects on children. The purpose of the session will be to explain how mediation and other available services to work. Then couples will decide for themselves if they want to use mediation. The information session will not be to discuss the details of their own personal circumstances.

Allegations of fault should no longer be used

At present the "ground for divorce" (the reason given to the court for seeking a divorce) is the irretrievable breakdown of the marriage. This can be proved by one of five "facts". Three are fault-based: adultery, intolerable behaviour, and desertion. The other two are: two years' separation with mutual consent, and five years' separation without mutual consent. Most people use the fault-based facts. Under these facts a divorce is often granted in less than six months and before arrangements for children, finance and property are settled. In other words, a system of divorce in which fault plays a part does little to bolster the institution of marriage. Allegations of fault are often exaggerated and unsupported. This often causes conflict, resentment, anger and bitterness, which last long after the divorce and are harmful to children.

Under the new system, the ground for divorce will remain the irretrievable breakdown of the marriage. This will be established by the passage of a fixed period of time. This should substantially reduce the acrimony and hostility in the current system.

There should be twelve months for reflection on whether the marriage can be saved

The Government has stated that it wants there to be an adequate period of time to test whether the marriage has genuinely broken down, and to enable the couple to consider whether their marriage can be saved. It has decided the period should be twelve months. During the twelve-month period the couple will have ample opportunity to seek help from professional marriage guidance or counselling organisations if they feel this would be useful.

Arrangements for children, finance and property should be settled before the divorce is granted

Marriage involves mutual legal obligations of support and sharing that other relationships do not. It is important to have laws which recognise and enforce these obligations in practical and realistic ways. The obligations arising from marriage cannot be ignored when a marriage has broken down.

Under the new system, during the twelve-month period the couple will have to consider these obligations and decide arrangements for children, finance and property before the divorce can be granted. The couple can take longer than twelve months to decide arrangements if necessary. Professional mediation services will be able to help with this.

Divorce should be barred where the dissolution of the marriage would cause grave financial or other grave hardship

The hardship bar exists to prevent dissolution of marriage in cases where it would lead to grave financial or other grave hardship for one of the couple. For all couples there is a bar on applying for a divorce during the first year of marriage.

Under the new system, the hardship bar will be retained, but will be available in all cases and not just in five-year separation cases as at present. The bar on applying for a divorce during the first year of marriage will also be retained.

Family mediation should be introduced

In family mediation an impartial third party, the mediator, helps the couple considering separation or divorce to meet to deal with the arrangements which need to be made for the future. Because the couple discuss these matters face to face rather than at arm's length through lawyers, family mediation is better able to identify marriages which can possibly be saved than is the legal process. If the couple believe there may be some hope for their marriage they can be referred to marriage guidance. Family mediation is more flexible than the legal process in meeting families' needs.

Family mediation helps the couple to reach their own agreed joint decisions about future arrangements. It improves communication between them. It helps the couple to work together on the practical consequences of divorce with particular emphasis on their joint responsibility to cooperate as parents in bringing up their children in the future, even when they are divorced. In family mediation the door is always open to saving the marriage.

Under the new system, couples will be encouraged to use family mediation to decide arrangements where mediation is appropriate. For eligible couples, publicly funded mediation, supported by legal advice as necessary, will be available. Mediation will not be compulsory. The Government has stated that it recognises that in some cases mediation will not be the best way forward.

Benefits for children

The proposals will have important advantages, according to the Government.

* They will help to minimise conflict, and so reduce the worst effects of separation and divorce on children.
* They will help and protect children by encouraging parents to focus on their joint responsibility to continue to support and care for their children in the future.
* They will encourage couples to meet the responsibilities of marriage and parenthood before the marriage is dissolved.
* They will allow couples to make workable arrangements through family mediation in respect of their children, home and other matters.

Summary

The Government has stated that it believes in the institution of marriage and the family. But it also accepts that marriages do break down. There is also a recognition that divorce is an important and sensitive subject on which many people hold strong views. In the Government's view these proposals will provide a means of achieving a divorce process that supports the institution of marriage, helps save marriages that can be saved, gives couples time to consider before making irreversible decisions, and minimises the trauma for the couple and the children.

It is expected that the reforms, or some of them at least, will take a minimum of twelve months to become law.

The Government's detailed proposals are set out in the White Paper entitled *Looking to the Future – Mediation and the ground for divorce*, available from branches of Her Majesty's Stationery Office, Command Number 2799, ISBN 0-10-127992-2, price £13.40.

USEFUL INFORMATION

This book is designed to give you as much information as possible and to prepare you for the legalities of the divorce procedure. There are many other sources of information about divorce and the various aspects of divorce such as welfare benefits, etc.

The **Citizens' Advice Bureau** is a very good source of advice. Other offices such as the **Department of Social Security** and the **Inland Revenue** are also particularly useful.

There are several organisations set up specifically to deal with divorcing and divorced couples. The most famous of these is **RELATE**, previously known as the Marriage Guidance Council. They provide skilled help from trained counsellors. They will not dictate what you should do and, if you decide at the end of the day to go your own way, they will advise you on the least painful way of doing so.

Please refer to Appendices A and B for a list of useful addresses.

APPENDIX A

USEFUL ADDRESSES – FAMILY

Courts Family Division
Principal Registry
Somerset House
Strand
London WC2R 1LP
Tel. 071 936 6000

Family Conciliation Service for
Northumberland and Tyneside
MEA House
Ellison Place
Newcastle Upon Tyne NE1 8XS
Tel. 091 261 9212

The Family Law Bar Association
Queen Elizabeth Building
Temple
London EC4Y 9BS
Tel. 071 797 7837

Family Mediators Association
The Old House
Rectory Gardens
Henbury
Bristol BS10 7AQ
Tel. 0272 500140

Family Policy Studies Centre
231 Baker Street
London NW1 6XE
Tel. 071 486 8211

Family Rights Group
The Print House
18 Ashwin Street
London E8 3DL
Tel. 071 923 2628

Family Service Units (offices nationwide)
207 Old Marylebone Road
London NW1 5QP

Family and Youth Concern
Wicken
Milton Keynes MK19 6BU
Tel 0908 57234

Gingerbread (Guidance for single parents and children)
35 Wellington Street
London WC2E 7BN
Tel. 071-240 0953

Grandparents' Federation
Room 3
Moot House
The Stow
Harlow
Essex CM20 3AG

Head of Family Law Division
Lord Chancellor's Department
Southside
105 Victoria Street
London SW1E 6QT
Tel. 071 210 2059

Institute of Family Therapy
Family Mediation Service
43 New Cavendish Street
London W1M 7RG
Tel. 071 935 1651

National Council for One Parent Families
255 Kentish Town Road
London NW5 2LX
Tel. 071 267 1361

The National Family Conciliation Council
Shaftesbury Centre
Percy Street
Swindon
Wiltshire SN2 2AZ
Tel. 0793 514055

National Organisation for the Counselling of Adoptees and Parents
(Norcap)
3 New High Street
Headington
Oxford OX3 7AJ
Tel. 0865 750554

National Stepfamily Association
72 Willesden Lane
London NW6 7TA
Tel. 071 372 0844
(counselling service tel. 071 372 0846)

Post-Adoption Centre
8 Torriano Mews
Torriano Avenue
London NW5 2RZ
Tel. 071 284 0555

RELATE Marriage Guidance
Herbert Gray College
Little Church Street
Rugby
Warwickshire CV21 3AP
Tel. 0788 573241

Reunite - National Council for Abducted Children
PO Box 4
London WC1X 8XY
Tel. 071 404 8356

Solicitors Complaints Bureau
Portland House
Stag Place
London SW1E 5BL

Solicitors' Family Law Association
PO Box 302
Orpington
Kent BR2 6EZ

Appendix B

USEFUL ADDRESSES – GENERAL

Lifeline Pregnancy Counselling & Care
The National Administrator
Cae Bach
4 Pant y Wennol
Bodafon
Llandudno
Gwynedd LL30 3D
Tel. 01492 543741

Mothers Apart From Their Children
(MATCH)
c/o BM Problems
London WC1N 3XX

British Association for Counselling
1 Regent Place
Rugby CV21 2PJ
Tel. 01788 578328

Citizens' Advice Bureau
National Association
115–123 Pentonville Road
London N1 9LZ
Tel. 0171 833 2181

Child Support Agency
PO Box 55
Brierley Hill
West Midlands DY5 1YL
Tel. 01345 133133 (Enquiry Line)

European Commission on Human Rights
Council of Europe
BP 431 R6
Strasbourg 67006 Cedex
France
Tel. 010 33 88 61 49 61

Foreign & Commonwealth Office
Consular Department
Clive House
Petty France
London SW1H 9HD
Tel. 0171 270 1500

General Register Office
(Births, Deaths & Marriages)
St Catherine's House
10 Kingsway
London WC2
Tel. 0171 242 0262
or
Smedley Hydro
Trafalgar Road
Birkdale
Southport PR8 2HH
Tel. 01704 69824

International Social Service of the United Kingdom (ISS)
Cranmer House
39 Brixton Road
London SW9 6DD
Tel. 0171 735 8941

Just Ask (Advisory and counselling service)
46 Bishopsgate
London EC2
Tel. 0171 628 3380

Law Centres Federation (offices nationwide)
Duchess House
18–19 Warren Street
London W1P 5DB
Tel. 0171 387 8570

The Law Society
113 Chancery Lane
London WC2A 1PL
Tel. 0171 242 1222

Legal Aid Board
29–37 Red Lion Street
London WC1R 4PP
Tel. 0171 831 4209

Life Cares (Pregnancy, birth, adoption, DSS benefits, facilities for disabled parents or children)
LIFE House
Newbold Terrace
Leamington Spa
Warwickshire CV32 4EA
Tel. 01926 421587

London Friend (Counselling and support for lesbians and gay men)
86 Caledonian Road
London N1
Tel. 0171 837 3337

National Association of Councils for Voluntary Service (NACVS)
3rd Floor, Arundel Court
177 Arundel Street
Sheffield S1 2NU
Tel. 0114 2786636

Office of Population Censuses & Surveys
(OPCS)
Smedley Hydro
Trafalgar Road
Birkdale
Southport PR8 2HH
Tel. 01704 569824

The Prince's Trust
8 Bedford Row
London WCLR 4BA
Tel. 0171 430 0524

The United Kingdom Passport Agency
Clive House
Petty France
London SW1H 9HD
Tel. 0171 630 1199

INDEX